Designing Classroom Research

Themes, Issues, and Struggles

Margaret Eisenhart
University of Colorado

Hilda Borko
University of Colorado

Allyn and Bacon
Boston • London • Toronto • Sydney • Tokyo • Singapore

Editor-in-Chief, Education: Nancy Forsyth
Series Editorial Assistant: Christine Nelson
Editorial-Production Service: Spectrum Publisher Services
Manufacturing Buyer: Megan Cochran
Cover Administrator: Linda Dickinson
Cover Designer: Suzanne Harbison

Copyright © 1993 by Allyn & Bacon
A Division of Simon & Schuster, Inc.
160 Gould Street
Needham Heights, Massachusetts 02194

Library of Congress Cataloging-in-Publication Data

Eisenhart, Margaret A.
    Designing Classroom Research: Themes, Issues, and Struggles/
Margaret Eisenhart, Hilda Borko
        p.   cm.
    Includes bibliographical references and index
    1. Action research in education.   2. Educational psychology—
Research.   3. Educational anthropology—Research.   I. Borko,
Hilda.   II. Title.
LB1028.24.E37   1993
370'.78—dc20   92-25466
                                                              CIP

Printed in the United States of America

10 9 8 7 6 5 4 3 2 1   97 96 95 94 93

Contents

Preface

In recent years educational researchers, like ourselves, and educational practitioners, like many of our students, have become increasingly interested in what actually happens in classrooms and why it happens. For most of us, the impetus for this interest is a desire to improve educational practice. Toward this end we have found that we need more comprehensive and more collaborative classroom research to inform decision-making about educational practice. This book is our attempt to coordinate what is known from previous classroom research—specifically, research that has been guided by educational psychologists and educational anthropologists—and to work toward ideas, commitments, and guidelines that can inform future educational research efforts. The book emphasizes: (a) how the social science disciplines of psychology and anthropology have informed classroom research; (b) how interdisciplinary collaboration and teacher-researcher collaboration can contribute to classroom research; and (c) how standards for assessing classroom research designs can be developed and applied.

We wrote this book primarily for graduate students in schools and colleges of education who are beginning a course of study devoted to understanding or producing educational research. As such, we anticipate that the book will be useful as one of a set of required readings, in courses such as Introduction to Educational Research, Introduction to Disciplined Inquiry, and Introduction to Educational Research Design, that introduce educational research and its design to master's-level and beginning doctoral students in education. In addition, the book has a place in more advanced courses specifically about classroom research—courses such as Research on Teaching, Research on Classroom Learning, and Classroom Research.

Potential users should note that this book is *not* about research methods per se; rather, it is about the larger context of constructing classroom research designs in which a variety of research methods might be used. However, throughout the book we rely on a small number of exemplary classroom studies—some completed, others on-going at the time of this writing—to illustrate our ideas about research design; in presenting these studies, we also illustrate how research methods fit into research designs. The methodological implications of our book could easily be drawn out and elaborated by using the book in conjunction with a methods anthology, such as the American Educational Research Association's (1988) publication, *Complementary Methods for Research in Education*, edited by Richard Jaeger. That anthology presents in detail the assumptions and techniques of numerous research methods used by educational researchers.

It is also important to acknowledge that we wrote this book to be a point of departure for discussions with novice researchers about educational research design. Thus, the book is not fully transparent in the tradition of introductory textbooks. It does not identify objectives for each chapter, list every key source, bullet major points, or provide study questions. Instead, it presents positions that can and should be scrutinized and debated by those who would become active consumers or producers of educational research. Thus, we expect and intend that the instructor will expand upon and perhaps dispute some of the positions we take.

Finally, in addressing this book to novice educational researchers, we have tried to take away some of the mystique surrounding research that can intimidate novices. One way we have tried to do this is to insert personal stories of our research experiences—including some of our faltering steps and difficulties—in the same book with a more academic presentation of our central concerns and ideas. This approach was risky for us. Most people, including reviewers and editors, do not expect to read personal stories in a book about research. Most people, including ourselves, do not have clear models for writing in ways that combine first and third person voices, although for some years now, critics of research and of academic writing have argued that the personal experiences and commitments of researchers are, in fact, part and parcel of their "scientific" research and should be recognized as such. In the absence of agreed upon ways of revealing the link between researchers' personal experiences and their work, we have devised one way to combine the personal with the academic.

Although some readers might find our approach disjointed or biased, we took the risk, and the book that follows is the result. We want to thank our former and current editors, Susan Willig and Carol Wada at Prentice Hall, Sean Wakely at Allyn & Bacon, and the reviewers of our manuscript—Laura D. Goodwin of the University of Colorado at Denver, Carla Mathison of the San Diego State University, Stephen Olejnik of the University of Georgia, Susan Brookhart of Duquesne University, Jerry Allender of Temple University, and George Johanson of Ohio University—for supporting us in this "experiment." We would also like to thank our friends and colleagues, Elizabeth Fennema, Alison King, Margaret LeCompte, Jan Nespor, and Terry Wood, for their reactions to portions of this book. Although they do not necessarily agree with our interpretations or arguments, they have been helpful critics throughout. Now, we look forward to your reaction.

To Alex and Graham,
with love and for the promise of education in their lives

▶ 1

Introduction

We are two educational researchers who have been conducting educational research, mostly in classrooms, for more than 15 years. Although we began our careers in different fields (Eisenhart as an educational anthropologist; Borko as an educational psychologist) and a continent apart (Eisenhart in North Carolina; Borko in California), since 1980 we have spent a great deal of time talking with each other about educational research, trying to collaborate on educational research projects, and thinking about how to make educational research stronger.

In some ways, this book is our story; that is, it is the story of our introduction to and training for educational research, and our subsequent efforts to work together, although we did not share either theoretical commitments or methodological expertise at the beginning. Our story runs through the text, but we highlight it in this chapter and the next. In other ways this book is an academic argument about educational research, specifically classroom research—a more formal presentation of what we have learned about the strengths and limitations of educational and classroom research from our own work and that of others. We develop our argument primarily in Chapters 3 through 8.

In most books about educational research, the authors are invisible yet omnipotent. They know everything about research design and technique; they rarely make mistakes; they never tell who they are or how they got to be so smart. In this book, we begin by making ourselves known, and in doing so we try to make our experiences with educational research come alive. For us, doing research has been hard, challenging, fun, time consuming, disappointing, and, in the final analysis, extremely rewarding. We hope this book permits us to pass on some of our struggles, insights, and enthusiasm for this activity. We begin by introducing ourselves.

EISENHART'S STORY

I applied to graduate school in anthropology at the University of North Carolina, Chapel Hill, in 1973. I did not choose UNC after a long and arduous search for the perfect graduate school; I was a North Carolina resident. To afford graduate school, I had to attend a school where I would be an in-state resident. I also did not have a very good idea how I would pursue my interests at UNC. From my courses in undergraduate school, I knew I wanted to combine anthropology and education in some way. No one at UNC at the time pursued such a combination. At that point, I did not know there was a subfield of cultural anthropology called Anthropology and Education, but I was encouraged by my undergraduate Anthropology professor, Gwen Neville Kennedy, and the chairman of the Anthropology Department at UNC, John Honigmann, to pursue my interests. Once enrolled in the UNC program, I decided I wanted to study what children learned about race and gender at school, from an anthropological perspective. Luckily for me, the following year the department hired a new professor, Dorothy Holland, who had some interests similar to mine. This event was completely serendipitous in my regard; the department hired her primarily for her expertise in a completely different subfield, quantitative research methodology.

From this rather inauspicious beginning, things began to improve. From Holland and from various readings, I began to learn something about Anthropology and Education. Over time I came to understand educational anthropology as a subfield devoted in a general way to a variety of research questions and methodological orientations that address the question, "Why is teaching and learning occurring in this way in this setting?"

Eventually, I even began to write about the subfield myself. I argued, based on ideas from cultural anthropology, that the general aims of educational anthropology are to identify the sociocultural processes that constitute education in a particular setting and to make sense of the processes through the development, modification, or adoption of theories of culture and social relations (Eisenhart, 1988). Educational anthropologists, like many other cultural anthropologists, have been trained to assume that human behavior and human learning are responsive to a context that is pervaded by patterns of culture and social relations which, in turn, are interpreted and reconstructed by the participants. An educational setting is viewed as an organization of meanings and social relations that tend to support the social order of groups within the society. Research activity focuses on describing educational manifestations of the cultural and social order and on elaborating or developing theoretical frameworks for understanding how students, through exposure to education, come to learn their place in society (Eisenhart, 1988).

I also learned ethnographic methods, but not the same methods some educational researchers might expect. Ethnographic methods are often considered the *sine qua non* of cultural anthropology and thereby of educational anthropology. Particularly in the educational research community, educational anthropology has been linked with ethnography and thereby to qualitative methodology; thus, ethnography tends to be contrasted with quantitative methodology. In my graduate program in anthropology, however, I learned ethnographic methods—the techniques of participant observation and open-ended interviewing—in conjunction with so-called "quantitative" methods such as surveys, quasi-experiments, and inferential statistics. In my training program, the idea was to learn about a range of methodological tools and then to select the most appropriate methods for acquiring information about sociocultural processes in a given situation.

I also learned that neither the assumptions nor the preferred techniques of ethnography have remained fixed or uncontested over time (Howe and Eisenhart, 1990). Clifford, for example, recently pointed out that ethnography has sometimes been used to describe, sometimes to explain, and sometimes—more recently—to interpret (Clifford, 1988). At times it has been fundamentally historical; at other times, ahistorical. It has emphasized external observations or alternatively insider interpretations. As I have recently demonstrated, methodological interests and priorities held over from the past are being challenged and in some cases giving way to new ones (Howe and Eisenhart, 1990). We will return to these issues later in the book. For now, let me continue with the story of my career.

In 1975, after writing my first major research proposal with Holland, we were awarded a grant from the National Institute of Education (NIE; now the Office of Educational Research and Improvement) to conduct a two-year ethnographic study of an elementary school that was in the process of desegregating from an exclusively white school to a school with 65 percent black students. We were primarily interested in how the meaning of "race" would be constructed and learned at this school where black and white students and teachers were, for the most part, new to each other. To gather data for this study, I spent two to three days per week at the school. Most of the time was spent sitting in the back of the three fifth-grade classrooms (1975–76) and then the sixth-grade classrooms (1976–77), writing descriptions of the social interactions among the students and between them and their teachers. Some time was also spent observing interactions on the playground and in the cafeteria, and conducting "open-ended"[1] interviews with students and teachers about such things as the words and phrases they used to describe each other, particularly members of the other racial group. I also attended PTA meetings at the school, interviewed parents in their homes, and observed at district school board meetings, in order to learn the views of people who affected the school but were not daily participants in it.

After two years of collecting data and another year of analyzing the more than 2000 pages of written notes and transcribed interviews, we reported our results to NIE. Our report and conclusions filled more than 500 pages (Clement [now: Holland], Eisenhart, Harding, and Livesay, 1978). In it we described in detail how fear of racial tensions and violence, coupled with uncertainty about how to deal positively with cross-race relations, led the school to paint a "veneer of harmony" over its racial tensions, thereby simultaneously denying that it had any racial "problems" and missing opportunities to correct the numerous racial misunderstandings that occurred (and lingered) at the school (Clement, Eisenhart, and Harding, 1979).

Then, needing to do something "original" for my dissertation and having already given four years of my life to this study, I decided to reanalyze the data to look for evidence of how the meaning of gender was constructed at the school, and to compare the meaning of gender to the meaning of race. This project took another two years and earned me my Ph.D. in 1980. In the gender reanalysis, I found that gender was an even more important differentiator *among the students* than was race. Also, although the teachers reacted somewhat differently to the specter of gender differences than to race differences—seeing gender differences as "natural" developments that teachers hoped would be left outside the school door rather than as "undesirable" indicators that might be labeled "discrimination"—many outcomes were the same; that is, the students were left on their own to work out the meaning of gender in their school activities, and they did so in conservative, i.e., gender stereotyped, ways (Eisenhart and Holland, 1983).

Up to this point in my career, I thought of myself primarily as an anthropologist. Although I was interested in schools and other educational settings, I viewed these places as the "sites" rather than the major focus of my research. I was not particularly interested in the kinds of things I assumed educators were interested in—instructional strategies, subject matter areas, and curriculum materials. In contrast, I was interested in the social knowledge that was being taught and learned in school. At the time, I considered the social and academic aspects of school to be separate phenomena. This was to change after I began my professional teaching career in a college of education and came to know Hilda Borko.

In the spring of 1980 I was offered a position as assistant professor of anthropology and education in the College of Education at Virginia Tech in Blacksburg, VA. I accepted and began work there that fall. Hilda Borko was also a new assistant professor at Virginia Tech that fall, and we soon became friends. Little did we know at the time how differently our training experiences had prepared us to conduct educational research and how much time we would spend trying to figure out our differences.

BORKO'S STORY

In comparison with Eisenhart, my career as an educational researcher began with much closer ties to the classroom and much less focused ideas about and commitments to the research enterprise. I graduated from the University of California at Los Angeles (UCLA) in 1971 with a Bachelor of Arts degree in psychology and without a clear image of my career path. However, coming from a family of educators (my mother was a high school teacher and my father a university professor), it was only natural to enter a teacher certification program. (In California at that time, as now, teaching certification programs were fifth-year programs, entered into after completion of an undergraduate degree.) I enrolled in an internship program at the University of Southern California (USC). I spent one year, full time, in an elementary school. In the mornings I was a student teacher, with placements in second- and sixth-grade classrooms and a class for mildly handicapped children. In the afternoons I was a teacher's aide in the Special Education classroom. I took classes at night, and at the end of the academic year I had earned a California State Elementary Teaching Credential with a specialization in Mental Retardation.

I realized during that year that I did not want to teach in a public school. Still uncertain about a career path, I applied to and was accepted into doctoral programs at both UCLA and USC. At USC I was accepted into the Special Education program and offered the opportunity to work with a professor who ran programs for delinquent youth. At UCLA my acceptance was in Philosophy of Education, with the opportunity to begin a private alternative school with a number of friends and colleagues whom I had met as an undergraduate student. I decided to accept the offer from UCLA, primarily because I wanted to be involved in the alternative school project. In Los Angeles, similar to many other places in the country in the early 1970s, there was a fair amount of dissatisfaction with the public schools. A small but growing alternative education movement was flourishing, and I wanted to be part of that movement.

I entered the Graduate School of Education as a Philosophy of Education doctoral student in 1972. The professor who served as my advisor, and who provided leadership for the alternative school project, was Carl Weinberg. For my first several years as a doctoral student, the formal educational program took a secondary position to other commitments. My first priority was University Middle School, the alternative junior high/high school that we created. To the extent possible, I took university courses in the late afternoons and evenings, so that I could spend the school days at University Middle School. Studying was relegated to evenings and weekends, and I was not involved in any research projects.

Early in my doctoral studies, I realized that my strengths and interests were in the area of educational psychology, not educational philosophy. That realization should not have come as a surprise, given my almost nonexistent undergraduate preparation in philosophy and my extensive background in psychology. I switched into the educational psychology program (at UCLA it was called Learning and Instruction). Eva Baker, head of the Center for the Study of Evaluation, agreed to be my temporary advisor until my research interests became clear (and to remain my advisor if my interests matched her own).

During the fourth year of University Middle School's existence, and my fourth year of doctoral studies, we made the decision to close the school. Many of us, myself included, were ready to move on to other things. My personal decision was based on a desire to devote more time and mental energies to my doctoral studies. I had begun to feel that I was missing out on too much by being away from campus so much of the time, and I had reached the point where I wanted to be a full-time student. I soon realized that to fully experience the role of a graduate student, I needed to become involved in the educational research enterprise. I also realized that my interests were not in the area of program evaluation. So, I began to search for a possible research focus and a professor with whom to work (a situation which is often quite anxiety-producing and that many graduate students face at some point in their careers!).

At that time, Richard Shavelson, who had been hired as a faculty member in Learning and Instruction and Research Methods a few years earlier, was looking for graduate students interested in working with him on research projects about teacher thinking. I was intrigued by the topic and (with some sense of relief) grabbed the opportunity to work with him.

Research on teacher thinking has a relatively short history in the field of educational research. The vast majority of work in this area has been conducted since 1976, approximately the time that I became involved in educational research. The roots of current research on teacher thinking can be traced back to a National Conference on Studies in Teaching convened by NIE in June, 1974, to create an agenda for future research on teaching. Ten panels were organized. Panel 6, "Teaching as Clinical Information Processing," was chaired by Lee Shulman. One of the experts on that panel was Shavelson. The report it produced argued for a program of research on teacher thought processes and provided a rationale for and assumptions underlying such a program:

> *It is obvious that what teachers do is directed in no small measure by what they think. . . . To the extent that observed or intended teacher behavior is "thoughtless," it makes no use of the human teacher's most unique attributes. In doing so, it becomes mechanical and might well be done by a machine. If, however, teaching is done and in all likelihood will continue to be done by human teachers, the questions of the relations between thought and action become crucial. (National Institute of Education, 1975, p. 1)*

Thus, panel members argued, to understand what is uniquely human about the process of teaching we must study teachers' thinking, for example, their planning and interactive decisions.

Looking back today, I am again aware of how fortuitously my career in educational research began. I was fortunate to have been introduced to Shavelson. And, I was fortunate that my interests were so well matched to his and to an emerging research area.

A small number of students, all working with Shavelson and all interested in teacher decision-making, formed a study and research group. One of our initial projects was a doctoral seminar in which we met weekly to discuss substantive and methodological issues in research on decision-making. As an outgrowth of that seminar, we began working on a set of related research studies that eventually evolved into a number of doctoral dissertations [several of which are described in Borko, Cone, Russo, and Shavelson, (1979)].

My dissertation study focused on teachers' judgments about students' academic achievement and behavior and their decisions regarding classroom organization and management. It used policy capturing, a method borrowed from laboratory psychology for studying human judgment and decision processes. In a policy-capturing study, the researcher attempts to identify the kinds of information subjects (in this case, teachers) use and the ways in which they integrate that information to make judgments and decisions. Typically, teachers are provided with a series of simulated cases or vignettes created by the researcher so that information about several features or "cues" is systematically varied. Mathematical models, usually linear regression models, are constructed based on statistical analyses of the teachers' judgments and decisions. The models describe the relative weightings that teachers attach to these cues when making judgments or decisions. Thus, these models are said to "capture" the teachers' decision policies.

In my dissertation, teachers read descriptions of hypothetical students who differed in gender, general achievement, rule-following behavior, ability to work independently, social competence, and self-confidence. They judged the likelihood that each student would master the skills and concepts typically included in the fifth-grade curriculum, would be highly motivated, and would be a behavior problem. They then made a series of decisions about appropriate classroom organization and management strategies for the students. In general, regression models with only one to three variables did a good job of representing teachers' decisions. However, when we (a colleague in the research group and I) compared regression models for individual teachers, we found individual differences in the information teachers used and the ways they used that information (Borko and Cadwell, 1982). This finding suggested that it was misleading to look across teachers for an average or typical decision policy.

Although policy-capturing research provided some insights into the teachers' thinking, I found myself disturbed by its limitations. For example, the regression models provide a picture of decision outcomes but say nothing about the decision process. We could not make inferences about why teachers pay attention to certain types of information more than others, or about how they integrate information from various sources to make pedagogical decisions.

My concerns about the methodology were reinforced by the frustrations that a number of participants expressed about the study. They complained that they wanted more information about the hypothetical students, and that some of the information they typically take into account in their own classrooms was unavailable in the experimental task. They also reported that the task seemed artificial, unlike their decision-making in actual classroom situations. These concerns led to an interest in exploring other ways of studying teachers' thinking. However, I am skipping two years in my story.

As I neared completion of my dissertation in the summer of 1978, I realized that I was not yet ready to leave the Los Angeles area. Although I was fairly certain that I wanted an academic position at a university, that option was not available as long as I was committed to staying in the Los Angeles area. So, I took a position at System Development Corporation in Santa Monica working on a project funded by the U.S. Office of Education to study the parental involvement components of federally funded educational programs such as Title I (now Chapter I) and Follow Through. The core group of professionals working on that project included a quantitative research methodologist, an educational sociologist, an educational anthropologist (Eisenhart was not the first anthropologist with whom I worked!), and myself—an educational psychologist. The project had two major components—a national survey of a sample of districts and schools with federally funded programs to collect demographic information and descriptions of the parental involvement components of their programs, and case studies of 60 districts and 120 schools, to collect in-depth information about parental involvement program components and activities. The project was one of the first (and, to my knowledge, the few) federally funded evaluation studies to use qualitative research methods. I worked with the sociologist and the anthropologist to develop interview and observation guidelines and analysis plans to be used at all 60 case study sites. I was also responsible for overseeing data collection at six Follow Through sites across the country, since we had hired local field researchers to collect the data and conduct preliminary analyses at each site. However, I left the project before its completion, to accept a position as an assistant professor at Virginia Tech.

I arrived at Virginia Tech in August, 1980, still committed to exploring teachers' thinking, dissatisfied with the research methods I had used up to that point, and with some experience using alternative methods in a very different context. Thus, I was open to exploring the different research assumptions and methods to which Eisenhart introduced me, although I had no idea of the time and mental energy we would spend trying to learn about each other's discipline.

WORKING TOGETHER[2]

Thus, our association began fortuitously, at Virginia Tech in 1980, when we were both brand new assistant professors struggling to design our own programs of research, to find the time and resources to conduct research, and (of course) to get it published. From the beginning, we realized we had a special relationship for our times. Borko was trained in cognitive psychology—the discipline contributing the most to educational research—and was well-connected to important figures in the educational research community. Eisenhart's degree was in anthropology, far from the educational research mainstream at the time, but with training and interests that put her in the midst of debates, beginning in the middle 1970s, about the diffusion of ethnographic methodology into mainstream educational research.

Also from the beginning we recognized that we stumbled over language and concepts as we tried to communicate our interests to each other. The assumptions and jargon of anthropology did not fit together easily with those of psychology. Where social processes intrigued Eisenhart, cognitive processing intrigued Borko. When Eisenhart wanted to interpret an individual's behavior in terms of group norms, Borko wanted to interpret it in terms of individual knowledge and thinking. However, we shared an interest in understanding teaching and learning in classrooms. This shared interest and our curiosity about each other's discipline led us to plan to do some research together.

In our first project together (Borko, Eisenhart, Hoover, Niles, and Wolfle, 1981), we set out to study the acquisition of reading in four second-grade classrooms. From the outset, we hoped to integrate understandings of classrooms from our two disciplines in order to obtain a more comprehensive picture of classrooms than we thought was possible from the standpoint of one discipline alone. The division of labor that emerged put Borko and Niles, a reading educator, in charge of developing research questions about the cognitive and instructional aspects of reading. Eisenhart worked on research questions about the social environments for reading in the classroom. Basically we ended up with a longer-than-usual list of research questions, because each of us was willing to simply add to the questions of interest to the other. We successfully completed the project (Borko, Eisenhart, Kello, and Vandett, 1984; Borko and Eisenhart, 1986, 1989), but our form of working together was, for the most part, to list important ideas from anthropology and from psychology and then to pursue research questions pertaining to each item on the list, using qualitative methods somewhat tenuously connected to the methods we had previously been trained to use.

Although this project constituted an "advance" for us because each of us was forced to consider the perspectives of the other discipline, it was not a very satisfactory collaboration. Basically we had two sets of interests that we pursued in the same study but not really in an integrated way, a fact reflected in our data-collection guidelines and analysis procedures as well as in our articles about the study. For example, in the earliest article (Borko et al., 1984) we examined teacher decision-making using the perspective of cognitive psychology. Then, in Borko and Eisenhart (1986) we used theoretical perspectives from anthropology to examine reading groups as a self-perpetuating system of student conceptions and behaviors, skills stressed by teachers, and reading activities. In Borko and Eisenhart (1989), we again used ideas from anthropology to examine the reading groups as literacy communities. The data we drew upon for the second and third articles did not overlap at all with the data presented in Borko et al. (1984). We look back on this research design now and want to call it "additive," rather than "collaborative."

More recently, we have embarked on an on-going joint project, this one investigating the process by which novice middle school mathematics teachers learn to teach. Many of the same issues have come up again but in a more complicated form because this time our team includes four mathematics educators as well as the two of us. We will use the example of this project later in the book to illustrate more about the research dilemmas we have faced and our attempts to resolve them.

REASONS FOR WRITING THIS BOOK

Our experiences talking and working together have made clear to us a number of important points about the research process—points that are not often mentioned in books on educational research; points that we want to stress in this book. First, educational research is almost always collaborative in some sense. That is, whether researchers interact face-to-face or more indirectly via articles, books, telephone, or computer, they depend on each other, on funding agencies, and on practitioners to help them formulate significant and timely research projects. Being willing and able to collaborate productively is, we think, an important part of successful educational research in general, and classroom research in particular.

Second, educational research is a complex activity that requires ongoing deliberation and decision-making. Educational researchers do not have recipe-like directions for how to do their work, nor do they always know from the outset of a study exactly what will be possible, what will happen, or what they will be called upon to do in order to complete the study. The need for deliberation and decision-making is especially obvious when the research team is comprised of people with different disciplinary backgrounds or different experiences of practice. Discussions among individuals with different backgrounds can be time-consuming and tedious and ultimately may require compromises by everyone; but they seem to us to be the best and perhaps only way to produce both credible and useful educational research. We hope to convey a sense of this process, both its inevitable messiness of false starts, reiterations, clarifications, and redundancies as well as the elation of discovery and innovation that can only come from the exciting possibilities produced by the conjunction of different minds and purposes.

Third, educational research is evolving; its designs and procedures are not cast in stone. Conscientious researchers are continually trying out new methods for capturing some feature of education; continually trying to make their work stronger, more compelling, and more useful. In educational research of the 1980s, qualitative methodologies, such as ethnography and case study, and mixtures of qualitative and quantitative methodologies have been proposed as additions to the storehouse of familiar quantitative research methods. More sophisticated quantitative methodologies, such as structural equation modeling and hierarchical linear modeling, have been proposed to address issues such as causal inferences and the analysis of multilevel (e.g., school, classroom, and student) data. In practice, the standards for using these "alternative" methodologies in educational research are not routinized in the same way they are for more established methodologies; thus, their use demands more thought and explanation than might be necessary if conventional procedures were used.

Our work together also has led us to identify a set of continually frustrating questions about the goals and practice of classroom research. In particular, we have come to question the usefulness of the conventional "specialist approach" to educational research as a model for classroom research. When, for example, educational psychologists investigate the amount of time that students spend on cognitive tasks in classrooms while educational anthropologists try to map the social relationships emerging among students and teachers, the result is often, and we think unfortunately, a fragmented view of what classrooms are like and how and why they function as they do. Although specialized investigations may lead to advances in the specialty area, they are often not comprehensive enough to provide the information necessary for teachers, administrators, and policymakers to implement changes of major educational importance. We wanted classroom research to become more comprehensive.

We also keep wondering why the findings from classroom research studies are so rarely translated into practice, either by teachers or researchers. One problem seems to be that the procedures for collecting and reporting data associated with conventional research designs make this translation difficult. Designs that demand standardized measures, true experimental treatments, correlational analyses of classroom variables, or surveys tend to obscure, rather than highlight, the inevitable mix of multiple factors that affect educational practice in any given school. They may also cancel out, by averaging the results for the sake of reporting and anonymity, the differences in attitudes and orientations among teachers. In the case of ethnographic or other qualitative methods, research results can be dismissed by teachers if studies report things that seem "obvious," have no clear practical implications, or are virtually impossible for teachers to change. Qualitative results may also be dismissed if teachers do not have time to read the often lengthy and tedious reports that qualitative researchers think they must produce in order to "explain" their findings.

As we came to appreciate the important role that these factors play in helping or hindering teachers and others to make desirable changes in their own classrooms, we had to question the general preference for conventional designs (of all kinds) in educational research. On the other hand, conventional designs have important strengths—policy-makers understand them; many people, from politicians to parents, are persuaded by them; and agreed-upon standards for conducting them exist—that new, alternative methods lack, at least at first. If some methods are not appropriate and the alternatives lack credibility, then educational researchers seem to be in a quandary about how to proceed. We wanted to find a way to move beyond the impasse.

Finally, and related to the preceding issue, we came to question the tendency for educational researchers to leave classrooms and schools as soon as research data are collected. Typically, educational researchers return to the university setting to analyze their findings and to write about their work for university audiences. They tend not to be engaged in efforts to apply, or use, the results of their research to improve educational practice in the sites of their studies. Unfortunately, when research results are described for university audiences, they are not easily translated into classroom practice, and their potential for educational improvement is greatly reduced. We wanted to encourage more educational researchers to commit themselves to educational change and improvement in particular schools or with particular teachers.

THE DESIGN OF THIS BOOK

In this book we present our ideas about classroom research from these starting points. The perspective we present has emerged from our work together, our reading of others' work in educational anthropology and psychology, and our discussions over the years with prospective teachers, experienced teachers, school administrators, university colleagues, parents, and students about classroom life.

In Chapter 2 we give our reasons for wanting to encourage research specifically in classrooms, and we discuss what we think are important shortcomings of previous classroom research. By outlining the strengths and weaknesses of previous work, we direct attention to the kinds of issues we think should be addressed in classroom research of the future and set the stage for developing the various components of our perspective. The key components introduced in Chapter 2 are a commitment to comprehensive studies through interdisciplinary collaboration, and a preference for research that produces locally sensitive and usable results for educational practitioners.

Chapters 3 and 4 continue, in a sense, the chronicle of our own training and commitments. One consequence of our first collaboration efforts was the realization that we each needed to be very clear about our respective disciplinary foundations; only with such clarity would we feel comfortable making decisions to compromise on one point but not on another, to leave one thing out but not another, as we tried to fit our research interests together. These two chapters describe the results of reviews that each of us undertook in our respective disciplines, in order to establish, for ourselves, the disciplines' contributions to classroom research. We begin, in Chapter 3, with contributions from cognitive psychology because we expect it will be the more familiar discipline to most readers. Then in Chapter 4 we turn to educational anthropology. In each chapter, we discuss themes that are widely represented in the work of scholars within the discipline, and we feature one exemplary study to illustrate the themes.

Chapter 5 begins our discussion of interdisciplinary collaboration in classroom research. In this chapter, we present in more detail our view of and position on this form of collaboration, and we describe how these have evolved for us over the ten years during which we have worked together.

Chapter 6 presents our ideas about why educational research has so infrequently been used by practitioners. Then, from the standpoint of that analysis, and drawing upon our own and other researchers' experiences collaborating with practitioners, we suggest how it might become more useful and usable.

Good classroom research, in addition to being used, must also be credible according to some accepted standards. In Chapter 7 we take up the credibility of educational research. Building on work by Eisenhart and Howe, we propose that adhering to guidelines for research that stress the overall comprehensiveness and value of the research will increase the chances that the findings will make sense, will contribute in a general sense to educational deliberation and policy-making, and can inform local practice (Howe and Eisenhart, 1990; Eisenhart and Howe, 1992).

Having established in Chapters 3 through 7 the criteria we consider necessary for good classroom research in the 1990s, in Chapter 8 we describe two recent classroom research projects that, though relatively small-scale and low-budget, meet most of our criteria. The studies we use (in this chapter as well as earlier ones) are certainly not an exhaustive list of exemplary classroom research studies. However, they were well-known to us and served our purposes well. They are also easily accessible to others to read and assess independently of our evaluation.

In Chapter 9 we summarize our ideas by proposing an agenda for classroom research in the 1990s. For the reasons we have given earlier and those discussed in more detail in the chapters that follow, we think that being involved in classroom research in the final decade of this century is a very exciting place to be. We look forward to engaging you in this project as we proceed through the pages that follow.

NOTES

1. "Open-ended" interviews are characterized by questions that permit the respondent to answer in whatever way she or he wishes. No possible answers (such as multiple choice items) are provided, and no time frame or coverage is specified for the answers.

2. This section was originally published in Eisenhart and Borko, 1991.

▶ 2

The Potential of Classroom Research

WHY STUDY CLASSROOMS?

Classrooms are obviously special settings for teaching and learning: the academic work and the social relationships that take place there determine much of what is taught and learned in school. In fact, it would not be unreasonable to claim that classrooms are *the* crucial context for formal education. To understand and improve what is taught and learned in schools, we must understand the academic tasks and social relationships that constitute the classroom learning environment. For this reason, classrooms are, and should be, sites of great interest to educational practitioners, policy-makers, and researchers.

More and more, educational researchers from diverse disciplinary backgrounds are spending time studying actual classrooms. Some want to explore in detail what really goes on in a classroom and why things happen there as they do. Others want to compare classrooms in order to understand alternative models for classroom organization and instruction. Still others want to try out new ideas in the classroom, to assess the potential for practical applications.

Despite these varied efforts, there remains much to discover about how classrooms are, or might be, organized for good teaching and learning, and about why they function as they do. For example, the myriad forces, including teachers, students, school administrators, parents, community, district, and society, that shape classroom life—their interrelationships and the constraints they impose on change—are not yet well-understood. Why is this the case? Our tentative answer to this question has to do with the characteristics of classrooms, the challenges that these characteristics pose for researchers, and the limited focus of most existing classroom research.

WHAT ARE CLASSROOMS LIKE?

Classrooms are distinctive places. As Doyle stated, "classroom settings have distinctive properties affecting participants regardless of how students are organized for learning or what educational philosophy the teacher espouses. There are, in other words, important elements already in place when teachers and students arrive at the classroom door" (Doyle, 1986, p. 394). These distinctive features include: 1) *multidimensionality*: the large quantity of events and tasks, multiple consequences of a single event, and many people with a broad range of social and personal objectives, that must be taken into account in classroom decision-making; 2) *simultaneity*: the reality that many things happen at once in classrooms, and that the teacher and students must attend to many things at the same time; 3) *immediacy*: the rapid pace of classroom events, providing teachers with little time to reflect before acting; 4) *unpredictability*: because classroom events are socially constructed, it is often difficult to anticipate how any particular activity will unfold; 5) *publicness*: events, especially those involving the teacher, are often witnessed by a large proportion of students; and 6) *history*: the accumulated set of shared experiences, routines, norms, and understandings that provide a context for classroom events. These intrinsic features of the classroom environment create constant pressures that shape the experiences of teachers and students alike. When the features of classrooms and the pressures they create are ignored by researchers, attempts to understand and/or improve teaching and learning are likely to be unsuccessful.

Classrooms are also complex places. Their complexity presents a challenge for teachers and researchers alike. As Good and Brophy argue, because of the fast-paced and complex nature of classroom interactions and communication patterns, teachers are often unaware of many classroom events (Good and Brophy, 1991). This lack of awareness sometimes results in unwise and self-defeating behaviors. Similarly, the constantly changing and complex nature of classrooms poses a challenge for researchers seeking to describe, understand, and/or improve classroom life. When their research designs do not take these conditions into account—for example, when designs focus narrowly on only one or two static aspects of classroom life—researchers run the risk of drawing inaccurate or inappropriate conclusions about what occurs in classrooms and why.

WHY IS IT IMPORTANT TO RECONSIDER THE DESIGNS OF CLASSROOM RESEARCH?

As a group, classroom studies appear to be a very mixed lot. They are derived from different disciplinary frameworks (e.g., psychology, anthropology, or sociology). They sometimes use the same abstract construct to mean different things (e.g., the somewhat different meanings of "cognition" in psychology versus anthropology). They rely on quite different analogies, e.g., the "classroom as factory" or as "system" in studies grounded in educational sociology, the "mind as computer" in cognitive psychology, the "classroom as theater" or "game" in educational anthropology. They use different research techniques, e.g., experiments or quasi-experiments that permit control but sacrifice "real life" versus ethnographies that examine real life but may include rather uncontrolled speculation about a given topic. And, they seem to pursue questions in a relatively unsystematic way, based on considerations such as sample convenience, political concern for ethnic and gender issues, and availability of funding for research on science and mathematics education.

This situation may be acceptable, even desirable, to disciplinary specialists such as the educational psychologist trying to extend or modify theories of human cognition, or the educational anthropologist trying to find innovative methods for discovering the classroom experiences of nonmainstream groups. However, it is probably not desirable if the goal is to understand the distinctiveness and complexity of classroom life. Because researchers in each discipline, and even in subdisciplines, use different theoretical lenses to study classrooms, they have usually investigated somewhat different topics or questions. Because what each group chooses to look at is different, what each finds tends to be different as well. Because each group's questions and findings are limited by the lenses and tools of its discipline, its research provides incomplete, and potentially misleading, pictures of classroom life. We wholeheartedly agree with Jackson's position:

> *Classroom life, in my judgment, is too complex an affair to be viewed or talked about from any single perspective. Accordingly, as we try to grasp the meaning of what school is like for students and teachers, we must not hesitate to use all the ways of knowing at our disposal. This means we must read, and look, and count things, and talk to people, and even muse introspectively over the memories of our own childhood. (Jackson, 1990b, xxi–xxii)*

From the perspective of a general audience with a desire to significantly improve U.S. schools, the present situation in educational research on classrooms is also undesirable. In addition to the potential risks of incomplete information and inaccurate conclusions, results reported within a discipline often are not disseminated to those in other disciplines. Sometimes results from different disciplines do not seem reconcilable. For these reasons, there tends to be little cross-disciplinary conversation or understanding. In addition, researchers do not, and in a real sense cannot, speak the same language when they discuss classrooms with each other or the public. These communication difficulties make the translation of findings into practice difficult.

Differences in the daily and immediate concerns of educational researchers and those of educational practitioners also are substantial. These differences set the stage for differences in the ways questions about classrooms are identified and in the ways solutions are proposed and implemented, thus contributing to additional communication and translation problems. Further, schools and school districts include different factions or groups of people with different beliefs about schools and what should occur there. These factions are the outcome of the social and political dynamics within the school, district, state, and country. Often, the researchers' results, when translatable into school- or classroom-related terms, appear to support the existing beliefs of some factions and challenge the position of others. Consequently, the research results may become a political football in a game that has little to do with the nature of the results or with educational improvement.

In short, although much work has already been done in and about classrooms, many important questions—important especially for the ways classroom research can or might be used—remain to be addressed. To best answer these questions, we think researchers must design studies that are sensitive to the distinctive features and complexity of classroom life, and compatible with the concerns of educational practitioners. In the chapters that follow, we will address, in more detail and in several different ways, all the issues raised above. For now, we return to the story of our own work which, in turn, will lead us to illustrations of how these issues have come up for us and how we have tried to address them.

OUR PLAN FOR OUR NEXT STUDY

As described in Chapter 1, we began conducting classroom research together in 1980. Since then, we have completed a classroom-based study of second-grade reading and written several papers about that study. More recently, we embarked on another study, entitled Learning to Teach Mathematics, which investigates the process of learning to teach middle school mathematics as it unfolded for a small group of novice teachers from the time they entered their final year of teacher preparation through their first year of full-time teaching. This time our research team includes two mathematics educators (Catherine Brown and Robert Underhill) as well as the two of us.[1]

In this study, we are explicitly trying to identify different sources of influence on the process of learning to teach mathematics and changes in that process over time. By attempting to integrate the interests of mathematics education, cognitive psychology, and educational anthropology in a single study, we also are attempting to develop a model for the coordinated and longitudinal study of the content-specific, psychological, and sociocultural aspects of learning to teach—a model that accommodates some of the complexity that characterizes classrooms and those who are learning to work in them. In this study, we are investigating three different kinds of classroom settings: the public school classrooms in which a small group of novice mathematics teachers did their student teaching (studied in 1988-89), the classroom sessions of a mathematics methods course taught by a university professor for the same group of prospective teachers (1988), and the first-year teaching classrooms of the same teachers the following year (1989–90).

As we (Eisenhart and Borko) began to formulate our ideas about the Learning to Teach Mathematics study, we realized that we were in danger of falling into the same "additive trap" in which we found ourselves after our first study. In preparation for the mathematics study, we agreed to study changes in the student teachers' knowledge, beliefs, and thinking, as well as the influences of the settings in which they learned to teach. However, each of us then began our planning for the study by making a list of the things we, as individual specialists, most wanted to investigate, and by designing a study using our own preferred methodological techniques.

Specifically, Borko was interested in the individual novice teachers and changes in their knowledge and thinking during their final year of teacher preparation and first year of teaching. Her disciplinary perspective directed her attention to several areas of investigation common to cognitive psychological research on teaching and learning: the knowledge and beliefs that constitute novice teachers' professional knowledge base (Shulman, 1987); their thinking before, during, and after classroom lessons (Borko and Livingston, 1989; Clark and Peterson, 1986); the interrelationships among their knowledge, beliefs, thinking, and actions (Putnam, Lampert, and Peterson, 1990; Shuell, 1986); and their progress in the acquisition of expertise (Berliner, 1989; Borko and Livingston, 1989). These interests and the tradition within cognitive psychology predisposed her to envision a methodology that would carefully assess and trace over time the knowledge, thinking, and actions of individual novice teachers.

Eisenhart was interested in the influence of settings on learning to teach mathematics. Given the nature of teacher education in the United States, two settings were particularly important: the university teacher preparation program and the public schools where the participants were student teachers or first-year teachers of mathematics. Her educational anthropology perspective directed attention to two aspects of these settings: the cultures of teaching and learning to teach (Eddy, 1969; Fuchs, 1969), and the social organization of teaching and learning to teach (Erickson, 1982; Hart, 1982; Lacey, 1977). Further, her anthropological training and experience predisposed her to favor a methodology of extensive participant observation in the two kinds of settings.

These two sets of interests guided our initial thinking about the design of the Learning to Teach Mathematics study. However, we quickly realized that specifying sets of distinct interests did not provide much direction for designing a coordinated or integrated study. In the terminology of educational research, we lacked a "conceptual framework;" that is, we lacked a coherent approach to the study, one that would serve as a guide for an integrated rather than an additive research design and interpretation of results.

With these concerns in mind, we considered how best to work out the needed conceptual framework. We realized that our success would depend, at least in part, on our respective abilities to clarify what we really needed to study as an anthropologist or psychologist. We found ourselves asking—and trying to explain to each other—what *really* makes a study "psychological" or "anthropological" in nature. This line of questioning was somewhat uncomfortable for us both. Having been trained in one discipline, we tended to take its tenets for granted. We found it hard to say, exactly, what our disciplines were fundamentally committed to, and thus hard to say exactly what we should not compromise in our efforts to coordinate or integrate our interests.

This situation led us to realize that we needed to go back to our disciplines for something of a refresher course. We decided to review the recent classroom research done within our respective disciplines, in order to better understand their contributions and differences. In the next two chapters, we summarize the results of our reviews, in order to expose the nature of the tensions and compromises we faced as we tried to develop an integrated conceptual framework for our classroom studies.

In our reviews, we relied on two sources of information: 1) a systematic perusal of articles on classroom research appearing in the *Anthropology and Education Quarterly*, the *Journal of Educational Psychology*, and the *American Educational Research Journal* from 1982 to the present;[2] and 2) unsystematic consideration of articles and books that have been especially useful to us. Under the rubric of "classroom research" were included reports of studies conducted in classrooms, mostly in the United States, theoretical discussions of constructs for the study of classrooms, and articles about factors outside or beyond the classroom that affect it. Each of us worked on the review of her own discipline with the goal of identifying major themes that organized recent classroom research. A second goal was to use the themes to understand what makes a classroom study distinctively "anthropological" versus "psychological" and, on this basis, to develop some explicit guidelines that could help us retain our disciplinary orientations in our work on mathematics teaching and also, hopefully, permit more integration than we had previously achieved.

NOTES

1. Two doctoral students in mathematics education, Patricia Agard and Doug Jones, later joined the resarch team.
2. We would like to thank Paul Deering for his help in collecting these review materials.

▶ 3

Contributions from Cognitive Psychology[1]

THEMES IN COGNITIVE PSYCHOLOGICAL RESEARCH ON CLASSROOMS

Borko's review reaffirmed cognitive psychology's central focus on individuals and their mental lives and her own commitment to understanding the role that individual teachers and students play in the classroom teaching and learning process. Cognitive psychologists use a variety of models to describe and investigate the mental lives of teachers and students, and they pursue numerous research agendas. For example, some focus exclusively on teachers' thought processes or on their knowledge related to teaching. Others explore students' mental lives—their acquisition of knowledge or their use of learning strategies. Still others conduct research that focuses simultaneously on teachers and students, on teaching and learning.

Despite this diversity, cognitive psychologists' investigations of classrooms share a number of assumptions and focal issues. Our discussion in this chapter emphasizes these commonalities. It is organized around five themes: the tendency to make *mental events* the focus of study; an assumption that knowledge, thinking, and actions are interrelated; the tendency to investigate how knowledge is organized and structured in the minds of individuals; the tendency to investigate the specific thought processes of students and teachers that facilitate classroom learning; and an assumption that the acquisition of expertise includes qualitative changes in knowledge structures, thought processes, and actions. To provide an illustration of these themes and how they are incorporated into cognitive psychological research on classrooms, we feature the Cognitively Guided Instruction (CGI) project, an exemplary study of the teaching and learning of mathematics in first-grade classrooms.

The five themes of cognitive psychological research on classrooms are interrelated, and it is impossible to discuss one without addressing the others. Thus the order in which we present them in this chapter is somewhat arbitrary. Also, because they are so interrelated, we present all five themes before discussing how they are interwoven in the design of the CGI project.

The Study of Mental Events

Cognitive psychology is the scientific study of mental events. It is concerned primarily with the contents of the human mind, e.g., knowledge, perceptions, beliefs, and the mental processes in which people engage, e.g., thinking, problem solving, planning. A basic assumption for most cognitive psychologists is that knowledge and thinking are internal to the individual mind (Putnam et al., 1990).[2] As Resnick noted, "The heart of cognitive psychology is the centrality given to the human mind and the treatment of thinking processes as concrete phenomena that can be studied scientifically" (Resnick, 1985, p. 124).

Most cognitive psychologists use an information processing model to represent human mental events. They assume that the human mind is essentially a processor of information, and they describe mental events in terms of transformations of information from input (stimulus) to output (response). Within an information-processing framework, the computer is often used as a metaphor to describe an individual's mental events. A typical representation of the human mind using this metaphor includes four components: sensory register, short-term (working) memory, long-term memory, and response generator. The power of the computer metaphor lies in its ability to generate hypotheses about how people receive information from the environment, process or transform that information, and use it as a basis for action.

A major difference between the computer and the human mind is that people have limited information-processing capabilities. For example, the work space in short-term memory can hold only a very limited amount of information [7 ± 2 units of information; Miller (1956)]. Because of this limitation, it is important to minimize the burden placed on working memory during an information-processing task. To minimize this burden, teachers and students, like all persons attempting to solve complex problems, construct simplified representations of problems, i.e., problem spaces, and then search through these problem spaces for permissible problem-solving moves. One goal of cognitive psychological research on classrooms is to identify and describe the general strategies or heuristics that students and teachers actually use to solve problems of learning from classroom instruction (Leinhardt and Putnam, 1987; Wilson, Shulman and Richert, 1987; Winne and Marx, 1987).

Knowledge, Thinking, and Actions

Virtually all cognitive psychologists share a fundamental assumption that an individual's knowledge structures and mental representations of the world play a central role in perceiving, thinking, and acting (Putnam et al., 1990; Shuell, 1986). Unlike behavioral psychologists, cognitive psychologists assume that teachers' actions do not directly determine what students learn. Rather, these actions are signals that provide guidance to students about effective ways to contemplate the content of lessons. Learning is influenced by these signals. However, the knowledge and skills that students bring to the learning situation, and the cognitive activities they pursue while engaged in classroom activities, are the major determinants of what they understand and acquire from classroom lessons (Doyle, 1978; Winne and Marx, 1982, 1987). (The overlap among the themes is clear in this explication of the "knowledge, thinking, and actions" theme; it is impossible to discuss the theme independently of assumptions about students' mediation of classroom learning.)

Similarly, teachers' thinking is directly influenced by their knowledge. Their thinking, for example their planning and interactive decision-making, determines their actions in the classroom and, therefore, the signals available for student learning.

To understand students' learning from classroom instruction, researchers must take into account the teacher, the student, and the instructional task. We must study teachers' knowledge systems; their thoughts, judgments, and decisions; the relationships between teachers' knowledge systems and their cognitions; and how these cognitions are translated into action. In addition, we must investigate the relationships among the knowledge and beliefs that students bring to the learning situation; their thought processes during instruction; their actions in the classroom; and the actions of the teacher. The next two themes focus on several key elements of these relationships: the knowledge systems and thought processes of teachers and students.

A Focus on the Structure of Knowledge

"Knowledge" is a key construct in cognitive psychological research, and one that is particularly relevant to understanding classroom teaching and learning. Cognitive psychologists agree that "the essence of knowledge is structure. Knowledge is not a 'basket of facts' " (R. Anderson, 1984, p. 5). The centrality of the assumption that knowledge is organized and stored in structures led Putnam, Lampert, and Peterson to suggest that "a basic, though overly simplified, definition of knowledge in cognitive theories" is that "Knowledge *is* the cognitive structures of the individual knower" (Putnam et al., 1990, p. 57).

A number of models for the representation and organization of knowledge in human memory have been developed by cognitive psychologists. For example, J. Anderson proposed a model in which declarative knowledge, "knowing that" something is the case, is represented in memory as interrelated networks of facts or propositions (Anderson, 1983). Procedural knowledge, "knowing how" to perform various skills, is represented as a system of productions, i.e., statements about how and under what circumstances an action should be carried out (Anderson, 1983). Another model is provided by schema theory (R. Anderson, 1984). A schema is an abstract knowledge structure that summarizes information about many particular cases and the relationships among them. People store knowledge about objects and events in their experiences in schemata or knowledge structures representing these experiences.

Both of these models are general in nature; that is, the structures and systems they propose are meant to be applicable to all domains of knowledge. In contrast, Shulman's theoretical model of components of teachers' professional knowledge (Shulman and Grossman, 1988; Wilson et al., 1987) focuses specifically on knowledge related to teachers and the teaching profession. As such, it is particularly relevant to classroom research. Shulman and colleagues hypothesized that teachers draw from seven domains of knowledge, or sets of cognitive schemata, as they plan and implement instruction: knowledge of subject matter, general pedagogical knowledge, pedagogical content knowledge, knowledge of other content, knowledge of the curriculum, knowledge of learners, and knowledge of educational aims. Their Knowledge Growth in Teaching research program traced prospective secondary teachers' acquisition of professional knowledge during their year of professional preparation and their subsequent use of this knowledge in their classroom practice. It focused primarily on two of the seven knowledge domains: knowledge of subject matter and pedagogical content knowledge.

Shulman and colleagues identified four dimensions of subject matter knowledge that appear to be important for teaching: substantive knowledge, syntactic knowledge, depth of knowledge, and orientation to subject matter. Substantive knowledge is knowledge of the key facts, concepts, principles, and explanatory frameworks in a discipline. Syntactic knowledge is knowledge of the rules of evidence and proof within a discipline. Orientation refers to a person's beliefs about what is most valuable to know in a discipline. Evidence from the Knowledge Growth in Teaching research program suggests that differences in teaching are related to differences in the character of teachers' subject matter knowledge along these four dimensions. For example, teachers with greater substantive knowledge in a discipline tend to provide conceptual explanations as opposed to purely algorithmic ones, and they engage students in open-ended discussions more frequently than do teachers with more limited substantive knowledge (Shulman and Grossman, 1988).

Pedagogical content knowledge, or knowledge of subject matter for teaching, consists of an understanding of how to represent specific subject matter topics and issues in ways that are appropriate to the diverse abilities and interests of learners. It includes "for the most regularly taught topics in one's subject area, the most useful forms of representation of those ideas, the most powerful analogies, illustrations, examples, explanations, and demonstrations—in a word, the ways of representing the subject that make it comprehensible to others. . . . [It] also includes an understanding of what makes the learning of specific topics easy or difficult: the conceptions and preconceptions that students of different ages and backgrounds bring with them to learning" (Shulman, 1986, p. 9). Pedagogical content knowledge is a domain of knowledge that is unique to the teaching profession. It is the domain that distinguishes teachers from other content specialists such as theoretical mathematicians, research scientists, and journalists. Further, research by Shulman and colleagues suggests that pedagogical content knowledge is relatively undeveloped in novice teachers and that it can be substantially influenced by teacher education programs (Grossman, 1989).

Teachers' and Students' Cognitive Processes

Another major focus of cognitive psychological research on classrooms is the thought processes of students and teachers. Cognitive psychologists share the assumption that certain thought processes or cognitive skills facilitate classroom learning. Their research attempts to identify these skills and to describe their use in classroom instructional events.

A key assumption about student thinking is that learners play an active role in acquiring new knowledge; they *mediate* between teachers' actions and instructional materials, and their own cognitive and affective outcomes. Learning occurs as they make sense of instructional events by using their existing cognitive structures to interpret environmental stimuli. It also occurs as they modify and elaborate their knowledge structures through a process of adaptation to the environment. Metacognition plays a key role in these processes. Successful students monitor what they do and do not understand during classroom instruction by asking themselves questions such as "Do I understand how to solve that problem?" or "What was the point of that example?" (Leinhardt and Putnam, 1987).

Leinhardt and Putnam developed a model of the skills a student needs in order to learn from classroom lessons by asking themselves the question, "What kinds of competencies would an elementary student have to possess to learn mathematics in the classroom of an effective math teacher" (Leinhardt and Putnam, 1987, p. 559)? Although derived from an investigation of mathematics teaching and learning, their model focuses on generic cognitive competencies. We feature it here because it is one of the most comprehensive models of students' learning from classroom lessons developed to date by cognitive psychologists.

The model consists of five major elements: an action system, a lesson parser, an information gatherer, a knowledge generator, and an evaluator. The *action system* is the set of competencies that enables the student to act appropriately in school. It contains a list of all the actions (generic and content-specific) that comprise the student's repertoire of "things to do in the classroom," as well as a component for recognizing when a particular action is being requested and one for learning new actions. The *lesson parser* is the set of competencies that enables a student to recognize and anticipate components of a lesson. It includes schemata for various types of lessons and their components, and competencies for recognizing and anticipating lesson segments. The third element in the model is the *information gatherer*. This set of competencies enables the learner to listen and watch selectively, and to sort incoming information on the basis of whether it should be retained as new information, retained as an elaboration of existing knowledge, or deleted. The main function of the *knowledge generator* is to process information gathered by the information gatherer. The learning mechanism, a major component of this element, learns the features of incoming information and makes sure that the incoming information is compatible with existing knowledge. The learner uses the information gatherer and knowledge generator in combination to "distill the essence of a lesson and learn from it" (Leinhardt and Putnam, 1987, p. 572). The final component of the model, the *evaluator*, performs the metacognitive functions of assessing the meaningfulness of incoming information and of monitoring the learner's understanding. Its primary role is to make sure that the new knowledge is being obtained from the lesson. All five elements of the model can be operating at any time and in any order. Leinhardt and Putnam claim that:

> . . . by understanding what the basic competencies are, we will be in a more powerful position to interpret some of the students' failures to learn and to help remedy those failures. [Also,] by understanding the core task demands, we can help teachers improve their teaching. We can develop a vocabulary that will let

us analyze how specific instructional weaknesses are likely to have an impact on student learning. (Leinhardt and Putnam, 1987, pp. 585-586)

Weinstein and Mayer proposed a taxonomy of generic learning strategies based on an extensive review of research on student learning (Weinstein and Mayer, 1986). Their taxonomy includes eight major categories of strategies: 1) basic rehearsal strategies; 2) complex rehearsal strategies; 3) basic elaboration strategies; 4) complex elaboration strategies; 5) basic organizational strategies; 6) complex organizational strategies; 7) comprehension monitoring strategies; and 8) affective and motivational strategies. They provide evidence that these sets of strategies enhance learning from classroom tasks and that they can be described and taught to students. They also offer a conceptual framework to guide the teaching of learning strategies to students.

A number of other researchers have explored cognitive strategies students use to learn from classroom instruction in specific subject areas. The two subject areas that have received the most attention are reading and mathematics. We explore some of the work in mathematics teaching and learning later in the chapter, through an examination of the CGI project. In the area of reading, a number of articles by Pressley and colleagues review and synthesize research on strategies that improve children's learning from text (e.g. Pressley, Johnson, Symons, McGoldrick and Kurita, 1989). Based on their review, Pressley and colleagues identify seven reading comprehension strategies, supported by research evidence, that they recommend should be taught to elementary school children: summarization, representational imagery, mnemonic representation, story grammar, question generation, question answering, and prior knowledge activation.

The student mediation perspective on learning from classroom instruction implies a role for the teacher that is different from the one typically envisioned in conceptions of teaching. Effective teachers help students to become actively engaged in learning activities appropriate for desired outcomes and to relate new knowledge to the knowledge they have already developed. They teach learning skills and strategies as much as, if not more than, specific content knowledge. "[G]ood teaching includes teaching students how to learn, how to remember, how to think, and how to motivate themselves" (Weinstein and Mayer, 1986, p. 315). These tasks require an awareness of the cognitive processes that the student must use in order to learn the content and an understanding of how prior knowledge and existing knowledge structures determine what and if the student learns from the material presented (Shuell, 1986).

The cognitive skill of "pedagogical reasoning" is central to this conception of teaching. As Shulman defined the term, pedagogical reasoning is the process of transforming subject matter "into forms that are pedagogically powerful and yet adaptive to the variations in ability and background represented by the students" (Shulman, 1987, p. 15). Pedagogical reasoning includes the identification and selection of strategies for representing key ideas in a lesson and the adaptation of these strategies to the characteristics of learners. Like pedagogical content knowledge, it is unique to the profession of teaching and is relatively undeveloped in novice teachers.

The Acquisition of Expertise

In recent years cognitive psychologists have attempted to unravel the nature of expertise by comparing the performance of experts and novices in cognitively complex domains such as chess (deGroot, 1965) and physics (Chi, Feltovich and Glaser, 1981; Larkin, McDermott, Simon and Simon, 1980). They have concluded that knowledge structures (cognitive schemata) of individuals highly skilled in a domain are qualitatively different than knowledge structures of novices. For example, cognitive schemata of experts are more elaborate, interconnected, and accessible than those of novices.

These differences in knowledge structures are associated with differences in the thinking and actions of experts and novices. For example, experts and novices differ in the ways they represent problems (Chi et al., 1981) and in the strategies they employ to solve them (Fredericksen, 1984; Larkin et al., 1980). Information that is useful for experts may hold little meaning for novices (deGroot, 1965).

One major focus of cognitive psychological research on classrooms is the development of pedagogical expertise. A number of researchers are attempting to understand and describe differences in the cognitive schemata, thinking, and actions of novice and expert teachers as they engage in classroom instructional tasks (Borko, Bellamy and Sanders, 1992; Borko and Livingston, 1989; Leinhardt and Greeno, 1986; Leinhardt and Smith, 1985). Others are tracing novice teachers' acquisition of professional knowledge and reasoning during preservice teacher preparation and the initial years of teaching (Feiman-Nemser and Buchmann, 1986, 1987; National Center for Research on Teacher Education, 1991; Shulman and Grossman, 1988; Wilson et al., 1987). Findings from this area of research suggest that characteristics of expertise identified in other cognitively complex domains are shared by expert teachers as well. For example, expert teachers notice different aspects of classrooms than do novices, are more selective and more efficient in their use of information during planning and interactive teaching, and make greater use of instructional and management routines. Many of these differences can be accounted for by assumptions related to several of the themes in cognitive psychological research—specifically, that novices' cognitive schemata are less elaborate, interconnected, and accessible than those of experts, and that their pedagogical reasoning skills are less well developed. [For a developmental model of pedagogical expertise that is related to, although not based upon, classroom studies of teacher cognition, see Berliner (1989)].

One implication of research on the nature of expertise is that novices, whether teachers or students, may not have the necessary knowledge and skills to adopt the complex pattern of activities displayed by experts in the classroom. We should therefore not attempt to educate novices by presenting them with information about how experts think and act and asking them to adopt those routines or actions. Instead, we should structure and sequence activities such that task demands are appropriate to the novices' level of readiness. Further, in the case of teachers, these activities should be designed explicitly to help novices develop and elaborate pedagogical content knowledge and pedagogical reasoning skills.

These five themes—the tendency to make mental events the focus of study; an assumption that knowledge, thinking, and actions are interrelated; the tendency to investigate how knowledge is organized and structured in the minds of individuals; the tendency to investigate the specific thought processes of students and teachers that facilitate classroom learning; and an assumption that the acquisition of expertise includes qualitative changes in knowledge structures, thought processes, and actions—have provided direction for cognitive psychological research on classroom teaching and learning. They have led researchers to examine the knowledge structures and cognitive and metacognitive processes that individual teachers and students bring to bear in classroom situations, and the role that these structures and processes play in the teaching/learning process.

METHODOLOGICAL CONSIDERATIONS

Cognitive research on teaching and learning has characteristic methods that differ from those used by researchers trained in other disciplinary traditions. These methods aim to provide data on thoughts, judgments, decisions, and other mental processes (Shavelson, Webb and Burstein, 1986). Although our book is not primarily about methods for conducting classroom research, we briefly discuss some of the most common methods used in cognitive research on teaching and learning, and we refer interested readers to other sources for additional information.

In their chapter on Measurement of Teaching in the third *Handbook of Research on Teaching*, Shavelson, Webb, and Burstein described the most commonly employed methods for measuring teachers' and students' cognitive processes, and they discussed issues related to the accuracy and consistency of the data obtained from these methods (Shavelson, et al., 1986). The methods they addressed can be placed in two broad categories—process tracing and regression modeling. Our discussion of methodological considerations begins with techniques subsumed within these two categories.

Process tracing refers to verbal report methods used to gather data on the cognitive processes people employ when solving problems, rendering judgments, and making decisions. The three most common process tracing methods are: 1) "think-aloud," in which a person voices her thoughts while performing a task such as reading from text, solving a problem, or planning a lesson; 2) "stimulated recall," in which a person thinks aloud while viewing a videotape or listening to an audiotape of herself performing a task; and 3) retrospective interviews, in which a person recalls thoughts after having completed a task. Shavelson and colleagues drew implications for evaluating the accuracy of process tracing data based on Ericcson and Simon's theory of verbal report data, and they compared process tracing methods on the basis of these implications (Ericcson and Simon, 1980).

Ericcson and Simon's theory is based on a psychological model of how people process information that uses the computer metaphor to represent the human mind (see the discussion of the computer metaphor earlier in this chapter). They hypothesized that data retrieved retrospectively from long-term memory (LTM) are considerably more limited than data retrieved from short-term memory (STM) because: 1) some of the contents of STM are lost in the transfer process to LTM, 2) data retrieved from LTM depend on the adequacy of search of LTM, and 3) persons may fill gaps in information retrieved from LTM by reconstructing or inventing data. They also hypothesized that when researchers constrain persons' reports of their thinking by using probes that request only certain information, they further limit the data by interrupting ongoing cognitive processes, encouraging reconstruction and filling in memory gaps, and increasing processing time (in the case of process tracing). Based on this theory, Shavelson and colleagues claimed that think-aloud methods theoretically provide the most accurate data on cognitive processes. Retrospective interviews are likely to produce incomplete and inaccurate data. Stimulated recall, although not as likely to produce complete, accurate data as concurrent (e.g., think-aloud) methods, provides an important alternative when it is not possible to have participants think aloud (e.g., during interactive teaching situations). Whatever method is used, probes should be general (e.g., "Tell me what you are/were thinking,") rather than specific (e.g., "Were you thinking of any alternative actions?").

Regression modeling techniques, such as "policy-capturing" and "lens-modeling," use statistical procedures to predict persons' judgments and decisions by identifying the kinds of information used and ways in which information is combined. The models generated by these techniques predict cognitive outcomes rather than modeling cognitive processes. They have been used to address questions such as the factors that predict teachers' judgments about students' academic achievement (Borko and Cadwell, 1982) and their selection of instructional materials (Byers and Evans, 1980). Regression modeling techniques typically have been used to study teachers' judgments and decisions using simulated cases or vignettes in laboratory studies rather than actual classroom situations (Borko and Cadwell, 1982; Floden, Porter, Schmidt, Freeman and Schwille, 1981; Shavelson, Cadwell and Izu, 1977). For the most part, they have not addressed the kinds of questions typically posed in cognitive research on classroom teaching and learning. [For further discussion of regression modeling techniques, see Shavelson et al. (1986)].

Shavelson and colleagues did not discuss observational methods for determining teacher or student cognition. However, although most early observational studies of classrooms examined the effects of teacher behavior and teacher-student interactions on student outcomes, a number of cognitive psychologists have recently begun to use observational data to draw inferences about teachers' and students' knowledge and thinking during classroom tasks (Leinhardt and Smith, 1985; Leinhardt and Greeno, 1986). To our knowledge, little has been written about criteria for assessing the accuracy or consistency of data obtained from classroom observational methods as sources of information on teacher or student cognition. Evertson and Green's chapter on Observation as Inquiry and Method in the third *Handbook of Research on Teaching* provides a useful framework for classifying classroom observational systems according to the nature of the system (e.g., closed versus open), types of systems (e.g., category, checklist, rating scales, narrative descriptions), methods of recording data, and general goals of the users (Evertson and Green, 1986). The chapter also discusses four research programs which were selected to represent different theoretical orientations and different observational approaches to the study of teaching-learning processes in educational settings. Although the chapter does not focus exclusively, or even primarily, on issues related to teacher or student cognition, it is an excellent starting point for researchers interested in exploring the use of observational techniques in classroom research.

These three categories of research methods—process tracing, regression modeling, and classroom observation—are not the only approaches to studying teacher and student cognition, although they are, perhaps, the most common. For another organizational framework for categorizing methods of research on teacher cognition, and for further description and critique of these and other methods (e.g., self-report scales and concept mapping) the reader is referred to Kagan's article in *Review of Educational Research* (Kagan, 1990).

THE COGNITIVELY GUIDED INSTRUCTION PROJECT: AN EXAMPLE OF COGNITIVE PSYCHOLOGICAL RESEARCH IN CLASSROOMS

In this section of the chapter, we describe the CGI project, a multiyear, multiphased program of curriculum development and research conducted by Thomas Carpenter, Elizabeth Fennema, and Penelope Peterson, and based on principles of teaching and learning derived from cognitive psychological research. We focus only on the initial two phases of the project, which were designed to investigate how teachers use findings from cognitive science research on children's mathematical knowledge and thinking to make decisions as they plan and implement instruction, and how this instruction affects their children's learning.[3] We selected the CGI project as an illustration in this chapter because it addresses each of the five themes to some extent. Further, because it focuses on both teacher and student cognition, it incorporates a broader range of assumptions and principles from cognitive psychology than do other, equally noteworthy classroom investigations.

We begin this section with an overview of the project. We then examine the extent to which it exemplifies the five themes in cognitive psychological research on classroom teaching and learning and addresses the methodological considerations related to examining cognitive processes.

An Overview of the Cognitively Guided Instruction Project

Phases 1 and 2 of the CGI project focused specifically on the teaching and learning of addition and subtraction in first grade classrooms. Phase 1 was a descriptive study in which the researchers attempted to identify and describe the relationships among first-grade teachers' knowledge and beliefs about students' mathematical knowledge and thinking, their reports of their approaches to teaching, and their students' achievement in mathematics (Carpenter, Fennema, Peterson, and Carey, 1988; Peterson, Fennema, Carpenter, and Loef, 1989). Phase 2 also examined teachers' pedagogical content knowledge and beliefs and their relationship to students' mathematics achievement. In addition, this phase included an experimental intervention, observations of the teachers' mathematics instruction, and additional assessments of their students' mathematical problem solving (Carpenter, Fennema, Peterson, Chiang, and Loef, 1989; Peterson, Carpenter, and Fennema, 1989).

Forty first-grade teachers participated in Phase 1 of the CGI project. They completed structured questionnaires and interviews that assessed their beliefs and knowledge about instruction, children's learning, and the mathematics content in addition and subtraction. The questionnaire and interview about teachers' beliefs were designed around four assumptions that underlie much of contemporary cognitive research on children's learning of mathematics: 1) children construct their own mathematical knowledge; 2) mathematics instruction should be organized to facilitate children's construction of knowledge; 3) children's development of mathematical ideas should provide the basis for sequencing topics for instruction; and 4) mathematical skills should be taught in relation to understanding and problem solving. The interview included questions to obtain specific information about the teachers' curriculum objectives, the roles of teacher and student in their mathematics classes, the content and techniques they used to teach addition and subtraction in their classrooms, and rationales for many of their responses. Instruments to assess the teachers' pedagogical content knowledge were based on a taxonomy of addition and subtraction word problems and children's solution processes, developed from cognitive science research on the development of addition and subtraction concepts and skills in young children (cf., Carpenter and Moser, 1983). The two measures of student mathematical achievement were a number facts test and a problem-solving test, both developed for the project.

Most teachers who participated in the study were able to identify many of the critical distinctions between different types of addition and subtraction problems, although they typically were unable to articulate why those distinctions were important. Almost all participants could characterize the primary strategies that children used to solve the different problem types. However, their knowledge generally was not organized into coherent structures in which distinctions between types of word problems, problem difficulty, and children's problem-solving strategies were related.

Differences in the teachers' pedagogical content knowledge and beliefs were related to their self-reported teaching strategies and to student achievement. For example, teachers with more cognitively-based perspectives (CB teachers) had greater knowledge of word-problem types and greater knowledge of their students' problem-solving strategies than did teachers with less cognitively-based perspectives (LCB teachers). They obtained this latter knowledge by observing their students as they solved mathematical problems during classroom lessons, rather than relying on tests or formal assessments. CB teachers made more extensive use of word problems in introducing and teaching addition and subtraction than did LCB teachers. They also placed less emphasis on the teaching of number facts, and they spent time developing children's counting strategies before teaching number facts. Children from both types of classes performed equally well on the test of addition and subtraction number facts; however, children in CB teachers' classrooms scored higher on problem-solving tests than did children with LCB teachers.

The major question addressed in the second phase of the project was whether knowledge derived from classroom-based research on teaching and laboratory-based research on children's learning would improve teachers' classroom instruction and students' achievement. The same group of 40 teachers participated. Twenty were randomly assigned to an experimental group and participated in a four-week summer workshop on Cognitively Guided Instruction. The remaining 20 teachers (the control group) participated in a half-day workshop on problem solving. Teachers and students were observed for 16 days of mathematics instruction during the course of the school year, using a coding system developed specifically for the project. Near the end of the year, teachers' pedagogical content knowledge was assessed by asking them to predict how individual students in their classes would solve specific problems, and then comparing their predictions with students' actual responses. They also were interviewed about their knowledge of their children's knowledge and about how they assessed and used this knowledge. Their pedagogical content beliefs were assessed using the questionnaire on children's learning of mathematics developed for Phase 1 of the study. Student achievement was assessed with standardized tests of computation and problem solving as well as the experimenter-constructed tests of number facts and problem-solving used in Phase 1 of the study. Students were also interviewed as they solved mathematical word problems to assess the cognitive strategies they used to solve different problem types. Finally, they completed several measures of attitudes and beliefs developed for the project.

The workshop for teachers in the experimental group was designed in accord with assumptions about teacher cognition and student cognition. Content of the workshop was based on the research on children's solutions of different types of addition and subtraction word problems. Format was based on the assumption that teachers are thoughtful professionals who construct their own knowledge and understanding (Borko and Shavelson, 1990; Clark and Peterson, 1986). Teachers were provided with access to knowledge about addition and subtraction problem types and the learning and development of addition and subtraction concepts and skills in young children. Time was set aside during workshop sessions for them to discuss principles of instruction that might be derived from the knowledge base, and they worked together and separately to design programs of instruction based on those principles. They were not *trained* in specific techniques for altering their teaching or their curriculum; nor were they provided with researcher-developed instructional materials.

Despite the fact that instructional practices were not prescribed in the CGI workshop, experimental teachers taught problem-solving significantly more and number facts significantly less than control teachers. Experimental teachers also posed problems to students more often, encouraged students to use a variety of problem-solving strategies, and more frequently listened to the processes used by students to solve problems. They believed that instruction should build on students' existing knowledge more than did control teachers, and they knew more about individual students' strategies for both number facts and problem solving. Experimental students exceeded control students in number fact knowledge and some tests of problem solving. They were also more confident of their abilities to solve mathematics problems and reported significantly greater understanding of the mathematics than did control students.

Some aspects of teaching and learning did not fit these general patterns. For example, CGI and control teachers did not differ significantly in their knowledge of students' problem solving abilities, as assessed by their predictions of students' performance on complex addition and subtraction word problems and on advanced problems. Also, both groups of teachers increased significantly in their agreement with the perspective that children construct mathematical knowledge and, at post-test, the two groups did not differ significantly in their agreement with this perspective. With respect to student achievement, CGI and control classes did not differ significantly in their achievement on the computation test or solving advanced problems.

A correlational analysis, using only data from the experimental teachers, provided additional insights into the relationships among teachers' pedagogical content knowledge, mathematics instruction, and student achievement. Teachers' knowledge of their own students' problem-solving abilities was significantly positively related to the teachers' questioning of students about their problem-solving processes and listening to students solving problems, as well as to the students' mathematics problem-solving achievement. This research suggests that experienced teachers' pedagogical content knowledge and pedagogical content beliefs can be affected by inservice workshops, and that such changes are associated with changes in their classroom instruction and with increased student understanding and problem solving in mathematics.

Cognitive Psychological Themes and Methodological Considerations

The assumptions and focal issues emphasized in cognitive psychologists' investigations of classrooms played a central role in the design and implementation of the CGI project. This role is immediately evident in the project's major research questions, which focus on the relationships among teachers' knowledge and beliefs, their classroom mathematics instruction, students' problem-solving strategies and their mathematics achievement. Mental events—both the contents and processes of the human mind—

clearly are featured in these research questions. Also prominent is the assumption that knowledge, thinking, and actions are interrelated.

A focus on the structure of knowledge is evident in the design of the research instruments and analysis strategies. For example, the questionnaire and interview to assess teachers' pedagogical content knowledge are based on a classification of word problem types and children's problem-solving strategies derived from cognitive science research. That classification system provided a highly structured framework for analyzing teachers' pedagogical content knowledge. Data-analysis strategies included the mapping of teachers' responses onto the framework. One major conclusion drawn in Phase 1 was that teachers' knowledge generally was not organized into a coherent structure that related distinctions between problem types, children's solution strategies, and problem difficulty.

The assumption that teachers' and students' thought processes facilitate classroom learning underlies both the content and the format of the CGI workshop. The format was based on the cognitive perspective that teachers are thinking individuals who approach teaching as a complex problem-solving task. Specific instructional practices were not prescribed for the teachers. Rather, workshop participants were provided with the resources and opportunities to design instruction based on principles of children's knowledge and problem solving, specific questions to address in their planning of instruction, and a great deal of freedom to monitor their own progress and to select activities that would facilitate their own learning.

A focus on children's thinking was apparent in both phases of the project, although it was more prominent in Phase 2. Content of the Phase 2 workshop for teachers was based, in part, on cognitive science research findings about the processes that children are likely to use in solving different addition and subtraction problem types. Assumptions about children's thought processes and their role in classroom learning also influenced data-collection strategies. For example, a problem-solving interview was developed to assess the strategies students used to solve the different types of addition and subtraction word problems. In addition, teachers were asked to predict the strategies that each of 12 target students in their classrooms would use to solve the same set of word problems. Analyses examined the relationships among teachers' predictions, students' problem-solving strategies, and students' achievement.

Acquisition of expertise was not an explicit focus of this research program. However, implicit in the orientation to students' learning of mathematics and teachers' learning of mathematics instruction is an assumption that changes in knowledge and thinking will be qualitative in nature. For example, the researchers expected that teachers would restructure their knowledge systems and would employ very different instructional strategies as a result of participation in the CGI workshop.

The CGI project focused primarily on the contents of the human mind, however not to the exclusion of attention to mental processes. In Phase 2 the researchers assessed the cognitive processes used by students to solve different addition and subtraction word problem types, as well as teachers' knowledge of those processes.

Information about specific data-collection instruments and procedures that is available in published journal articles and book chapters is limited. For example:

"[T]arget students were interviewed to determine the strategies they used to solve certain problems and to assess their recall of number facts. . . . The problem-solving interview consisted of six addition and subtraction word problems involving simple joining situations and missing addend situations with the change unknown" (Carpenter, Fennema, Peterson, Chiang, and Loef, 1989, p. 514).

Although it appears that a think-aloud approach was used, we cannot be certain. Nor do we have information about the nature of the probes used. However, these limitations are largely a function of constraints inherent in writing journal-length articles. Restrictions on length typically preclude researchers from providing all of the methodological detail that readers might want in order to understand the complex procedures used to study teacher and student cognition.

SUMMARY

In summary, cognitive psychologists conducting research on classroom teaching and learning have focused on the knowledge structures and cognitive and metacognitive processes that individual teachers and students bring to classroom situations. Using process tracing and observation methods, they have examined the role that these structures and processes play in the teaching/learning process. The results and conclusions of cognitive psychological classroom research focus on the cognitive skills and strategies of teachers and students that facilitate learning from classroom instruction, and on ways of helping individual teachers and students to acquire and improve these skills and strategies.

NOTES

1. Portions of this chapter and the following two have been adapted and expanded from Eisenhart and Borko, 1991.

2. There is a growing but still small movement within cognitive psychology to question this assumption. Rather than viewing knowledge and thinking as existing solely within the mind of the individual, proponents of this movement consider cognition to be interactively situated in physical and social contexts. For an introduction to this movement, see Putnam, Lampert, and Peterson (1990).

3. In the third year of the project, researchers conducted a series of case studies of six teachers who had participated in the original CGI workshop (Carpenter and Fennema, in press; Fennema, Carpenter, Franke, and Carey, in press). The goal of the case studies was to better understand the nature of the changes they had found in the experimental study. Current work in the CGI project has expanded the mathematical content domain to multiplication and division, place value, and geometry. For more information, a complete bibliography of writings about CGI is available from Thomas Carpenter or Elizabeth Fennema at the University of Wisconsin's Center for Education Research.

▶ 4

Contributions from Educational Anthropology

THEMES FROM CLASSROOM RESEARCH
IN EDUCATIONAL ANTHROPOLOGY

Eisenhart's review strengthened her commitment to view classrooms in terms of culture (collective beliefs, norms, and traditions) and social organization (arrangements of people, tasks, resources, and rewards that order activities within a setting), not in terms of individuals. Put another way, rather than focusing on patterns in the characteristics of individuals in classrooms, she was interested in the ideas and meanings promoted in classrooms and in how classrooms "work" as social units. To her, questions of special interest are: What meanings and ways of acting are being presented and promoted in the classroom or school? How do these meanings and ways of acting reproduce or challenge ways of thinking and acting that are prevalent in the larger society? How do they define the classroom context for teaching and learning? How do individuals and subgroups in classrooms and schools respond to the cultural and social features there?

Educational anthropologists, like cognitive psychologists, use numerous theoretical models and methodological procedures to investigate culture and social organization.[1] Here we discuss five themes that are widely distributed in the classroom research conducted by anthropologists of education. These themes are the tendency to make classroom or school *culture* the focus of attention; the tendency to view school social organization in terms of three distinct but interrelated contexts, the tendency to demonstrate that shared school situations do not produce the same responses in all students, an assumption that multiple perspectives are necessary to appreciate the complexity and variety of what is taught and learned in schools, and a dedication to using ethnographic research design as the primary tool for investigating classroom or school culture and social organization.

The Focus on Culture

First and foremost, cultural anthropology is the study of culture, and educational anthropology is the study of culture in educational settings, especially schools and classrooms. To understand how educational anthropologists study culture in schools, it is first necessary to review anthropologists' ideas about culture.

From the beginning of cultural anthropology as a discipline (near the end of the nineteenth century) until the 1950s, most anthropologists viewed culture as a bundle of features characteristic of a group of people with obvious boundaries and a distinct way of life. Each group was thought to be a coherent whole; that is, its various features were thought to fit together in an integrated way, thus providing a mutually reinforcing, consistent context for the group's activities including those associated with teaching and learning (growing up).

The assumed basis for integration of all the features of a culture was either a shared commitment to certain values or a particular subsistence pattern. When the integration was conceived of in terms of values, all the institutions of a society—its educational system, religious system, economic system, and social system—were thought to be undergirded by the same set of values. For example, Benedict, in her famous work, *Patterns of Culture* (1934), described how the value of individualism characterized aspects of the Plains Indian lifestyle and thereby distinguished them from the Pueblo Indians whose lifestyle was organized around values of communalism (see also M. Richardson, 1990).

Others thought that integration depended primarily on the subsistence pattern (or in complex societies, the "economic base") that the group used to survive (maintain itself) in its environmental circumstances. Both the social organization of a group's institutions and the content of its ideological systems were thought to derive from the base and to function in such a way as to support and maintain the base (Steward, 1955).

These two perspectives did not necessarily clash; in many ways they represented a difference of emphasis. A cultural group identified by and contrasted to other groups in terms of its values could also be a cultural group identified by and contrasted to other groups in terms of its subsistence base and the distinctive features derived from it. However, debates did ensue over which explanation was the more powerful, particularly for explaining why some groups maintained their culture while others were assimilated or even died out. Debates also raged over the best way to define culture (Kroeber and Kluckhohn, 1952). Despite such debates, a widely-held, general understanding of culture as "the lifeways of a group," including its distinctive values and subsistence pattern, emerged over time in the course of anthropologists' work.

From today's standpoint, these theoretical perspectives left some things out. Rarely, if ever, was the role of history, the effect of differential power distribution, or the influence of nearby or overlapping groups made explicit. In retrospect, these early theoretical perspectives seem idealized, romantic, and somewhat naive. But they reveal two important commitments still held by educational anthropologists. One is cultural relativism—that all cultures are created equal in the sense that they are coherent, i.e., internally sensible and reasonable to those who live in them. The second is cultural difference—that differences between cultures are profound and systemic, therefore translations from one cultural group to another can be very difficult to make and the potential for cross-cultural misunderstanding is great.

When culture is studied in educational settings in the United States, it tends to be for the purpose of explaining why children from nonmainstream groups—the culturally different—are less successful in school, on average, than mainstream children. One explanation for the discrepancy in school achievement is discontinuity between the nonmainstream beliefs, behavioral styles, and communication patterns expected at home and the mainstream beliefs, behavioral styles, and communication patterns expected at school. Anthropologists have theorized that if these differences go undetected, children from nonmainstream groups will have trouble understanding what is expected of them in school. Detailed studies of native Hawaiian community life, for example, have revealed how patterns of social relations and communication differ from those expected at the public schools attended by the children. Once the differences are understood, adjustments to bridge the gap can be made, children and teachers can achieve more effective communication, and more success at school can be expected (Boggs, 1985; Jordan, 1985; Vogt, Jordan, and Tharp, 1987). Similar studies have been conducted with American Indians (Philips, 1983), American Blacks (Heath, 1983), and Hispanics (Moll and Diaz, 1987).

Other Uses of "Culture"   Although an orientation toward culture that focuses attention on the beliefs and patterns of behavior that children bring to school is common, there are alternatives. One alternative focuses on the cultures that children develop in and around school (Eisenhart, 1989; Eisenhart and Graue, in press). These cultures do not necessarily form along ethnic, minority, or community group lines. Instead, the cultures of schools develop around divisions such as academic proficiency (Borko and Eisenhart, 1986), popularity (Eder, 1985), romantic relationships (Holland and Eisenhart, 1990), or commitment to mental labor (Willis, 1977). These studies make clear that familiar indicators of cultural difference—skin color, native language, religious or ancestral background—are not the sole determinants of the behaviors, attitudes, and performances of students. Group boundaries and cultural orientations emerge in and around schools, organized around the factors that are or become salient there. For example, some children arrive at school with little that differentiates them, yet the school's policies of assessment, grouping, and ranking may create its own set of groups and orientations toward school and school work [see, for example, Borko and Eisenhart, (1986)]. Groups formed at school also may divide ethnic or minority group members in different ways than do families or communities. And the cultural orientations of a school group may encourage members to think about school and act at school in ways that distinguish them from their ethnic counterparts (for example) in other school groups. Further, similar cultural orientations toward school can be produced in more than one ethnic group, such that members of various ethnic groups come to share similar orientations toward school. This alternate view of culture in schools and classrooms is a more expansive and complicated view because some of its features derive from ethnic, class, or linguistic traditions outside the school, while other features develop in and around the school itself (Eisenhart and Graue, in press).

In turning to the second theme—the tendency to view school social organization in terms of three constituent levels, we find that, in educational anthropologists' eyes, cultures—whether at school or outside it— cannot be understood without also understanding the contexts in which these cultures form and persist.

Three Constituent Levels Organize School Culture

Erickson's (1982) framework for the study of "taught cognitive learning" provides a starting point for presenting this theme. In his article, Erickson proposed that an adequate account of teaching and learning in school requires investigation of three semipermeable levels: 1) the general sociocultural system outside the school (consisting of customs, language, ideology, and social stratification inherited from previous generations), 2) the immediate learning environment in the school (consisting of the arrangement—both institutionally and interactionally induced—of people, time, space, resources, skills, and knowledge for face-to-face exchanges for teaching-learning), and 3) individual functioning at school (including cognitive processing, personal constructs, and self-image).

Although it is certainly possible to proceed with classroom research by parceling these three levels out to specialists, this is not what Erickson had in mind. Rather, Erickson argued that the three levels are mutually constitutive, inextricably interrelated, and should be studied as a whole. However, Erickson further proposed that the relationship among the levels be conceived as follows: the individual is connected to the wider sociocultural level through socially and politically patterned face-to-face interactions with older, more experienced members of a social group in an immediate learning environment. Although there is some "room" in this theoretical position for individuals to be active participants, anthropologists have historically tended to think of individuals as responding to the influences of the other two levels, rather than actively constructing or opposing them. In other words, individuals are viewed generally as "overdetermined" by the influences of the wider sociocultural system and the immediate learning environments in which they participate.

Erickson attempted to deal explicitly with the assumption that the meanings and social organization of classroom life, as well as the knowledge acquired there, are more than individual or even on-site productions. He argued that classroom life cannot be understood only by reference to what goes on in individual heads or in the classroom itself. On one level, classrooms are organized and infused with meaning from historical, political, and social forces outside classroom and school walls. The knowledge and behaviors taught and learned in the classroom are marked, inextricably then, by the social and political history of the society and by the structure and organization of schooling as an institution. These forces help to define and organize what is available for individual students and teachers to learn from their experiences of schooling. For anthropologists, school knowledge is not a domain of "subject matter" that can be separated from the sociopolitical context in which it has historically been used and continues to be used. Knowledge is always marked by its situations—past and present—of use (Cazden, 1989). Thus, research about classroom teaching and learning must be informed by understandings of how aspects of the wider sociocultural system are represented in classroom meanings and activities.

Further, immediate learning environments are constituted by social and political (as well as cognitive) activities for the people there. That is, what is actually taught and learned in the classroom emerges partly from the dynamic of social and political negotiations in which groups in a given classroom or school define their relationships with each other by using the material and symbolic resources available in school activities. Groups of people at school jointly and often implicitly develop "'working agreements' or 'consensuses' about who they are and what is going on between them, agreements which they formulate, act upon, and use together to make sense of each other" (McDermott, 1982, p. 252). Once established, these agreements can take on a life of their own, which may or may not correspond closely with those of the wider sociocultural system. Thus, the cultures, social groups, and relationships that exist in a particular school or classroom cannot be assumed a priori: the boundaries of groups, the resources (knowledge, skills, rights, obligations, and power) considered appropriate for group members to have or display, and the norms of the groups are locally produced and, in various respects, can be locally specific (Eisenhart, 1989; Willis, 1977). Fordham and Ogbu found, for example, that the black peer group in the high school they studied interpreted school activities in racial terms (Fordham and Ogbu, 1986). Speaking standard English, being in the drama club, making good grades, and getting high scores on standardized tests were interpreted as "acting white". Other activities, such as being good at sports and cutting up in class, were interpreted as contrary to acting white, and thus were viewed as more desirable for someone who is black. Black students who acted "white" in school risked being ostracized by their black peers. To avoid being shunned, many chose not to learn (at least, not to demonstrate in school) the skills and knowledge that would have made them appear to be "white" [see also Willis (1977) and Eckert (1989) for similar examples of school-related interpretations, constructed in terms of social class]. To understand what goes on in a given school or classroom, then, requires that its on-site cultures and sociopolitical organizations, as well as externally derived sociocultural constituents, be identified.

On Erickson's third level (individual functioning), prior experiences of individuals and their personal interpretations of school contribute to what is taught and learned. However, individuals' contributions are relatively minor. As indicated earlier, what is learned by individuals is thought to depend primarily on what is provided, and how it is provided, by the wider sociocultural system and the immediate learning environment. Individuals are generally not thought to possess or grasp culture or social organization in their entirety but to experience them partially and to respond to them in some way. The personal experiences of some individuals are well expressed by the cultures around them, and they rather comfortably find a place in one or more social groups. Others must search for cultures and groups (Eisenhart, 1990). A few never find cultures or groups in which they feel at home. Thus, most individuals behave or act the way they do—rationally or normatively—in response to the social and cultural surroundings in which they find themselves or place themselves. In other words, and in contrast to the psychologists' view, if anthropologists find an individual's actions to be "off-task," "lazy," "careless," "disabled," or "crazy" in a classroom, they will tend to look for the stimulus in cultural or group processes (and not in individual heads or personalities).

In sum, the second theme encourages a three-tiered approach to the study of classroom culture and social organization. From this perspective, influences of the wider sociocultural system, coupled with those of the immediate learning environment, have the most constraining effect on what is taught and learned at school. Of secondary importance are the influences of an individual's cognition and prior experiences.

Shared School Situations Do Not Produce the Same Responses in All Students

A third anthropological theme is that the situations of classroom and school life do not produce the same responses in everyone. For example, children of ethnic or class minorities often have different interpretations of the value of doing well in school than their mainstream peers. The third theme is clearly evident in the anthropological work that focuses attention on the background differences that children bring to school. These researchers have consistently demonstrated that linguistic and social differences in the ways children are raised at home lead them to experience the school environment in very different ways. Ogbu, although beginning from a theoretical position that stresses the economic barriers to good jobs for U.S. minorities rather than their background differences, has argued that many American Black and Hispanic children learn not to believe in the supposed link between good performance in school and a good job later (Ogbu, 1974). Because they (and their parents and friends) so rarely see evidence that people like themselves acquire "good" jobs, they are not encouraged or motivated to do well in school. Just "getting by" may be sufficient when school attendance and performance are thought to produce no clear benefit for students like themselves (see also Holland and Eisenhart, 1988). About this Ogbu has more recently written:

> The real issue[s] in school adjustment and academic performance . . . [are:]
> whether . . . the children come from a segment of society where people have traditionally [had trouble using] their academic credentials in a . . . meaningful
> and rewarding manner; . . . whether . . . the relationship between the minorities
> and . . . [those] who control the public schools has encouraged the minorities to
> perceive . . . school learning as an instrument for replacing their cultural identity with the cultural identity of their "oppressors" without full reward or assimilation; and . . . whether . . . the relationship between the minorities and the
> schools generates the trust that encourages members of the minorities to accept
> school rules and practices that enhance school success (Ogbu, 1987, p. 334).

For these reasons, following Ogbu, certain minority groups will have very different experiences of schooling than their mainstream peers.

Also even within minority groups, some students may do well while others do poorly. In other words, the link between group membership and school experience is not necessarily direct. In a 1988 article Weisner, Gallimore and Jordan emphasized that the wider sociocultural system—what they call "culture"—should be conceived as a set of opportunities or alternatives, available for individuals to use or not, rather than a fixed set of constraints that anyone raised in or belonging to a group must accept [see also Eisenhart (1989); Erickson, (1987)]. Weisner and colleagues wrote:

> Culture is not a nominal variable to be attached equally to every child, in the same way that age, height, or sex might be. Treating culture in this way assumes that all children in a culture group have common natal experiences. In many cases, they do not. The assumption of homogeneity of experience of children within cultures, without empirical evidence, is unwarranted. . . . The method error that follows is to measure culture by assigning it as a trait to all children or parents in a group, thus assuming culture has uniform effects on every child. (Weisner et al., 1988, p. 328; emphasis in original)

The same could be said about gender or class. Although researchers have often found that girls interpret the meaning of school experiences differently than do boys, gender does not always or consistently differentiate the responses of individual girls and boys to schooling (Eisenhart and Graue, in press; Holland and Eisenhart, 1988). Similarly, social class membership does not consistently differentiate school responses of individual students. In Willis' study of working-class high school boys in England, he found that some of the boys (the "lads") developed an antischool culture while others (the "ear'oles"), from virtually the same working-class background, developed a conformist culture (Willis, 1977). Further, the organizational arrangements of classrooms—which bring together and group children in different ways than do families or communities—may provide an arena for the construction of "new" meanings for school experiences based on joint activity in the regular classroom (Colleta, 1976), in ability groups (Borko and Eisenhart, 1986), or in cooperative learning groups (Deering, 1989; Jacob, 1989). In brief, the in-school experiences of students cannot be consistently predicted by characteristics of the group or groups to which they belong. Their experiences, like those of groups themselves, must remain open for investigation in a given school setting.

Multiple Perspectives

Anthropologists have long recognized two analytic viewpoints on cultural phenomena: the view of the cultural insider who understands the behaviors and ideas that have meaning to the people who regularly participate in the setting; and the view of the cultural outsider, usually the researcher, who is able (and interested) to observe, think about, and pursue evidence according to canons of rationality and science that persons immersed in a group would rarely use on themselves. The outsider view is likely to reveal patterns in group life that individuals enmeshed in it do not see; the insider perspective is likely to reveal the ways of thinking, the strategies, and the motives of insiders that would probably not otherwise be recognized by an outsider.[2] Although the anthropological community has often emphasized or focused special attention on one or the other perspective, it has also consistently tried to incorporate the strengths of each into its analytic frameworks. Applying these ideas to classroom studies has meant attempting to gather data from both the insider and outsider perspectives and to understand the relationship of the two.

Recently, the idea that culture is the temporary (constantly changing) product of "multiple voices," "narratives," "texts," or "dialogues" [see Cazden, (1989), Quantz and O'Connor, (1988), Tobin, Wu and Davidson, (1989)] has gained momentum in educational anthropology. A corrective to the assumption that consistent or shared insider or outsider views exist, this idea admits that within a social institution (a society, a school, etc.) various members or groups may have different and competing narratives of their worlds. In particular, people with power, or with the ability to influence those in power, are likely to give voice to things differently from those without power or access to it. As a further corrective to the assumption that such cultural differences are simply the consequence of minorities not understanding the "rules" of the institution, these competing voices are viewed as inevitably constituting the institution, providing through their interactions, negotiations, and conflicts the potential for reproducing the status quo or transforming it. This view emphasizes the need to collect and analyze data such that the multivocality within institutions can be revealed and preserved, and its potential for change and equality illuminated.

> *A multivoiced [study], with its presentation of both dominant and other voices, should provide an approach that offers a more accurate rendition of the complex relations of cultural life. Moreover, by recognizing and recording the multiple voices occurring within communities, we should be able to analyze the specific factors which affect the formation in historical situations of legitimated collusions and subsequent social actions. (Quantz and O'Connor, 1988, p. 99)*

Dedication to Ethnographic Research Design

Ethnographic research design is the methodology most commonly used by educational anthropologists. Theoretically, ethnographic design permits researchers to obtain direct access to cultural and social influences by involving themselves personally in the settings being studied. When using a classic ethnographic design, the researcher participates actively, observes personally, and interviews face-to-face in the environments under investigation. Using these techniques, he or she is expected to experience, as study participants do, the constraints and possibilities of culture and social organization.

In 1982, Spindler proposed a list of "criteria for a good ethnography," in the classic sense (Spindler, 1982). His criteria included the following: observations must be contextualized, prolonged, and repetitive; hypotheses, questions, and instruments for the study should emerge as the study proceeds; judgments about what is most significant to study should be deferred until the orienting phase of the field study has been completed; participants' views of reality are revealed by inferences drawn primarily from direct observation and various forms of ethnographic interviewing; sociocultural knowledge—both implicit and explicit—that participants bring to and generate in social settings should be revealed and understood (Spindler, 1982, pp. 6–7).

Although numerous ethnographers are currently adapting or modifying "classic ethnography" to suit their research purposes [see, for example, Cain (1989), Roman (1989), and the discussion of these two modifications in Howe and Eisenhart (1990)], the form outlined above is still generally used as the standard for accepted practice within the field.

WAYS WITH WORDS: AN EXAMPLE OF RESEARCH IN EDUCATIONAL ANTHROPOLOGY

To provide evidence of these themes and to demonstrate their use in an exemplary study, we showcase the ethnography, *Ways with Words: Language, Life, and Work in Communities and Classrooms* by Shirley Brice Heath (Heath, 1983). This ethnography has been widely read and well-received by both educational anthropologists and educational researchers from other disciplines and areas of inquiry. Although not the kind of study that most novices would feel comfortable undertaking, it stands out as an inspiring illustration of educational anthropology in practice.

We begin with an overview of Heath's study, to illustrate the character of a research study in educational anthropology and to provide a contrast with our earlier presentation of the Cognitively Guided Instruction project. Following the overview, we discuss the extent to which Heath's study reflects the five themes of research in educational anthropology.

An Overview of Ways with Words[3]

In the first part of the book, Heath reports the results of nine years of work living with, learning about, and comparing black working-class children in

Trackton, white working-class children in Roadville, and middle-class children, both black and white, living in the larger town of Gateway (all are fictitious place names) in the southeastern United States. Heath found distinctly different patterns of using language, interacting socially, and coming to understand one's place in society in the home environments of the three communities.

In Trackton, Heath found that life was a continuous bustle of social interactions with no fixed schedules or formal routines. Children learned that gaining the attention of others requires that they be entertaining and creative in their use of language. Parents were not interested in their children's rote learning of words and phrases; rather they emphasized the need for youngsters to learn to transfer verbal performances from one situation to another, to recognize when to say what, and to gain control of an audience through language use. Children were rewarded for being creative and innovative in their story telling, and from a very early age Trackton infants learned to assume the roles and guises of others as they recounted many a compelling story. The type of questioning that predominated in Trackton homes was heavily dependent on analogical reasoning skills: Children were asked questions such as "Now, what you gonna do?" or "What's that like?" Adults demanded, in response, creative and often witty answers, and they provided no exact standards for correctness. For Trackton parents, these linguistic skills were considered necessary for children to "make it" on their own in the world.

Children in Roadville grew up in a very different environment. Here strict eating and sleeping schedules were enforced for children, and children were carefully taught how to use words correctly from birth. Parents spent much time giving directives to their children; their questions were predominantly ones that encouraged or tested for the referential meaning of words and for knowledge of facts already known to the speaker—questions such as, "What is this?" or "Where is that?" Special attention was given to telling the truth, i.e., not telling "stories" that departed from the facts.

Clearly, the cultures that Trackton and Roadville children participated in before entering school were quite different, despite their geographic proximity. In addition, Heath found that middle-class children from Gateway displayed yet another set of cultural patterns. From infancy, Gateway children were seen as conversational partners by adults. Thus they learned to listen and respond to others. Gateway children were asked predominantly "What is it?" questions that demand referential knowledge (as were children from Roadville); however, Gateway children were also taught to link old information to new information, and to search for creative solutions (in this way, they were unlike Roadville children and more similar to Trackton children, although Gateway children were given more structured experiences for acquiring information than Trackton children).

When they began school, children from both Roadville and Trackton entered a world whose "ways with words" were distinctly different from what they had learned at home. Initially Roadville children were able to perform adequately because the school rewarded their learned ability to follow rules, to give the referential meanings of words, and to tell the truth. However, as the children grew older and the school began to demand imaginative thinking—a merging of reality and fantasy—Roadville children were quickly confused as school rules began to conflict with what they learned in their homes, i.e., to always tell the truth.

Trackton children, on the other hand, were well-practiced in the skills of imaginative thinking when they began school, but the format of the classroom—the stringent rules about the use of space and time, the demand for exactitude, and the emphasis on correct answers—baffled these creative entertainers. Heath described how the Trackton children would insist on trying to take the floor during story time (as they would do at home), and how teachers saw this initially as a lack of "normal manners" and later as evidence of "behavior problems." Over a period of time, the communicative differences between Trackton children and the "mainstream" children and teachers led most of the former to be labeled "potential reading failures," despite the incredible interpretive and linguistic skills evidenced by the same children at home.

After tracking the school progress of the children in her study, Heath found that success in school was closely associated with community membership, and thus with community culture. Middle-class students from Gateway did best at school, followed by those from Roadville and then by those from Trackton.

In concluding the report of her research, Heath stressed that what young children know about language and its use is learned as part of the interactional/communicative routines of the group in which they grow up. Early (home) social environments shape the way children grow up to understand the world by providing them with particular ways of thinking and patterns of behavior by which they learn how to make and take meaning. The ways of thinking and behaving may be quite different from community to community. Parents, community members, and later teachers distribute information through particular cultural channels, only insofar as they know how to "give" it, and students are able to acquire the knowledge presented only insofar as they know how to "take" it. If significant differences between ways of giving and ways of taking go undetected or unaddressed, exchanges of information are likely to be haphazard or unrewarding, and the best intentions of parents, teachers, or students may go unrealized. Only when early patterns of learning are consistent with, or can be attached to, those used in the schools are children likely to benefit from the instruction provided there.

In the second part of *Ways with Words,* Heath described how she and some of the teachers in the community schools used her research tools and her findings about the children's home cultures as a stimulus for redesigning their classrooms. Heath had wanted the teachers to be able to use her work, and they did. In doing this, the teachers aimed to "play to the children's strengths" (based on what the children had already learned and were interested in at home) so as to better teach them what they did not already know. For example, several teachers tried to create learning environments tailored to the very different cultural experiences of the children attending their school. One teacher, "Mrs. Gardner," began her year with a class of nineteen black first-graders—all labeled "potential failures" on the basis of reading readiness tests. Angered that "these children were designated 'no chance of success' before [even] entering school" and armed with Heath's findings, Mrs. Gardner set out to change things by searching for ways to connect her students' at-home experiences to the requirements of the school program (Heath, 1986, p. 286).

After learning exactly who would be in her class, Mrs. Gardner visited the communities that fed into it, jotting down such features as store names and streets, churches, and the location of street lights and telephone poles in the areas. Noting that several parents worked in local garages, she called them up and asked them for old tires, which were then cut up and used to make letters of the alphabet. Her curious requests got several parents intrigued, and soon many came to the school to help her construct the letters which were then scattered just outside the classroom.

As the semester began, Mrs. Gardner attempted to introduce the alphabet to her students, not merely as symbols on paper, but also as structured shapes apparent all over their neighborhoods. Children were asked to search for the big T's (telephone poles), to find the O's and the A's in such things as cups and saucers, tires, and street wires. They were also instructed to look for these shapes on license plates. As they became familiar with the shapes, Mrs. Gardner introduced the associated letter sounds—first by concentrating on the letters that began each child's name, and then by having children recognize certain sounds in words heard throughout the day. Next children used advertisements to separate lower-case from upper-case letters, and then match them. Mrs. Gardner also took pictures of her students that were then used to illustrate such concepts as "over," "under," "higher," and "lower."

At the end of their first year, by studying with a teacher who used creative teaching activities tailored for these black children, all but one child (who was later placed in a class for the emotionally handicapped) were reading at least on grade level—with eight at third-grade level, and six at second-grade level! Mrs. Gardner's efforts to make classroom learning an integral part of the lives of the students—based on Heath's research—

allowed previously "doomed" individuals to reach outstanding levels of competence.

Heath also described the efforts of "Mrs. Pat," who—following Heath's example—taught her students to be ethnographers. Most of Mrs. Pat's students came from poor farming families—35 percent of them black, and the rest white. The first step Mrs. Pat took was to try and show the relevance of school skills to the wider context of these students' lives. To this end, she contacted parents, community members, the principal, lunchroom workers and other students, and had them come to her second-grade classroom to talk about their ways of communicating, to explain how and why they used reading and writing, and to show the children samples of their writing and reading materials. Before every meeting, Mrs. Pat prepared her students to act as ethnographers—"detectives"—focusing on language in this case, by having them listen for answers to the following questions: What sounds do you hear when _____ talks? What did _____ say about how he talked? What did _____ write? What did _____ read? At the same time, children were exposed to a variety of literature—dialect poetry, radio scripts, comics, biographies of famous baseball heroes, in conjunction with the traditional basal readers and workbook exercises. Students became familiar with a variety of language data, thereby learning more about the situational use of language, as well as the differing attitudes toward it. They learned the difference between dialect and standard language, and between casual, formal, and conversational uses, i.e., the difference between oral and written traditions. "Throughout the year, the entire focus of the classroom was on language, its 'building blocks' in sound and in print, the ways its building blocks were put together, and how these varied in accordance with speaker and use in print or speech" (Heath, 1983, pp. 330–331).

Not surprisingly, by the end of the school year, Mrs. Pat's class had developed an amazing vocabulary, and many ways of talking about language. They had also come to see school reading and writing as connected to activities in the wider world: "Learning to read and write in school was now linked to reading and writing labels and bills in the country store, the cafeteria worker's set of recipes, the church bulletin, or a notice of a local baseball game" (Heath, 1983, p. 333). Children had gained a sensitivity to, and understanding for, the linguistic differences between people from all walks of life. Most importantly, however, these second graders now identified themselves as readers and writers.

Themes of Educational Anthropology *in* Ways with Words

Heath's study of socialization and schooling clearly focused on culture; specifically it focused on the cultures that children learned at home and brought to the school. Like other educational anthropologists using this orientation toward culture, she was concerned primarily with the way early experiences in the home generate patterns of thinking and behaving that may or may not correspond to those encountered or required at school. Heath demonstrated how the communicative patterns and norms taught in the home organize knowledge and mediate the way it is acquired in school.

Erickson's approach to the three levels of social organization also is represented in Heath's work, although her lens is trained on these levels as they affect (primarily) community, rather than school, life. Heath described the linguistic, social, and economic legacy inherited and enacted by each community. She also described in detail the immediate learning environments of family, neighborhood, and play groups in each community. Consistent with Erickson, Heath's portrayal of individuals was limited. Although they appeared in the book, they did not stand out from their cultural experiences; rather they exemplified the force of those experiences.

The third theme—that shared school situations do not produce the same responses in all students—is clearly evident in Heath's work. She found that linguistic and social differences in the ways children are raised at home lead them to experience the school environment in very different ways.

Regarding the fourth theme (multiple perspectives), Heath attempted to distinguish and integrate insider and outsider perspectives in two different ways. First, she separated her book into two parts. In Part I, entitled, "Ethnographer Learning," she adopted the stance of an "unobtrusive ethnographer," carefully recording but not disrupting the natural course of events in each community. In other words, in this part, she attempted to present the world of each community as insiders view it and live it. In Part II, "Ethnographer Doing," Heath became an "intrusive ethnographer" who intervenes in the workings of the schools and communities she has studied in hopes of improving the educational opportunities for the children. Here she presented the world of schooling and reform as she would like them to be, given an in-depth understanding of the communities served by the schools and a commitment to the goals of schooling.

Second, in both parts of the book, she quoted verbatim from participants and in this sense let them "speak for themselves," while also separating her words from theirs. But as in most classic ethnographies (and despite the two-part division of the text), it is Heath, not the people studied, who classified, organized, and ultimately interpreted the meaning of participants' words and actions. In other words, the perspective conveyed in Heath's book is primarily that of the outsider/ethnographer whose interpretations surround excerpts from insiders as recorded in fieldnotes and interview transcripts. Presumably her interpretations are imbued with empathy gained from her own in-depth, long-term involvement in the lives of participants, and informed by her knowledge of social science and educational concepts and theories. To the extent that she tacked back and forth between these two systems of meaning to develop her final interpretations (which we cannot determine from the information Heath provided in her text), she has written an account that is informed by both perspectives. Although Heath's procedures for accommodating insider and outsider perspectives are consistent with ethnographic tradition, recent critics of these procedures have questioned how adequately they permit multiple perspectives to be aired [in general and in Heath's work specifically, see DeCastell and Walker (1991)].

Heath's study in *Ways with Words* is an ambitious example of the use of ethnographic research to illuminate educational issues. From the text, we know that Heath adopted a participant/observer role in selected families in Trackton, Roadville, and to a more limited extent in Gateway. She also conducted many face-to-face interviews. She spent a long period of time studying the communities—nine years, and we can infer, although we cannot be certain because Heath does not say explicitly, that the course of her study—including the precise role she played, the questions she asked, the instruments she used, and the ideas that informed her work—was modified as she learned more about each community from her increasingly informed vantage point as an insider.

Before leaving this topic, we should point out that the lack of methodological detail provided by Heath also has generally been accepted practice among ethnographers. Until quite recently within anthropology, ethnographers have assumed or trusted that anyone who trained in the discipline and who demonstrated that he or she had spent a considerable amount of time living or participating with an unfamiliar group of people could and would conduct a competent ethnography. Especially with the importation of ethnography into other fields such as educational research, demands have increased on ethnographers to explain clearly and in detail the features of their methodology (Goetz and LeCompte, 1984). We will take up the issue of how to import methods from other disciplines for educational and classroom research purposes in Chapter 7.

SUMMARY

In summary, educational anthropologists working in the United States have focused specifically on culture and social organization and have primarily investigated the ways they are manifest and constituted in schools and classrooms, using ethnographic methods. They have explored multiple levels by which cultural traditions and norms, especially those derived from the wider sociocultural system (i.e., from outside the school), and social arrangements, especially those that characterize the relations between groups and individuals within the school and classroom, form part and parcel of what groups and individuals learn to do, think, and know in and about schools. In so doing (and in contrast to cognitive psychologists), the results and conclusions of anthropologists' studies stress the constraints imposed on individuals by external (rather than internal, psychological) circumstances and discuss primarily the social knowledge and the socially-situated actions (rather than the academic knowledge and the cognitively-guided actions) that are learned in schools and classrooms. Regardless of exactly how the significant contexts of education are conceived or exactly how the various participants contribute to and take meaning from them, the fundamental anthropological principle is that all teaching and learning is culturally bound and context dependent.

NOTES

1. The work of educational anthropologists has been informed by on-going exchange and lively debate with qualitative sociologists of education. For this reason, the research conducted by members of the two groups is sometimes indistinguishable and frequently cross-referenced. Two of the authors cited in this chapter—Paul Willis and Leslie Roman—are educational sociologists whose work is widely used by anthropologists. [For discussions of the similarities and dissimilarities of ethnographic research done by anthropologists and sociologists, see Goetz and LeCompte (1984) and Van Maanen (1988)].

2. Note that from this standpoint, the anthropologist's commitment to both an insider and outsider perspective is not exclusively a positivist or an interpretivist position; neither is it exclusively a quantitative or qualitative one.

3. Part of this description of Heath's work is adapted from Eisenhart and Cutts-Dougherty (1991), and reprinted by permission of the publisher from Hiebert, E. H., *Literacy for a Diverse Society: Perspectives, Practices, and Policies*. (New York: Teachers College Press © 1991 by Teachers College, Columbia University. All rights reserved).

▶ 5

Interdisciplinary Collaborative Research

WHAT DOES IT MEAN FOR RESEARCHERS TO COLLABORATE?

Much has been written recently about the value of collaborative research on classrooms. Calls for collaboration take several different forms. One call is for collaboration among educational practitioners and educational researchers; here, the aim is to bring together the expertise of the practitioner with the different expertise of the researcher, in order to more consistently and productively address practical educational problems (Atkin, 1989; Glickman, 1985; McDonald, 1989; Scriven, 1986). We address this issue in Chapter 6. Another call is for collaboration among educational researchers who have different perspectives on educational issues. Most often, this second call has been made in reference to research methods; that is, researchers are urged to move past debates about "methodology"—quantitative/qualitative; prescriptive/ descriptive; experimentalist/naturalist (Garrison, 1986; Howe, 1988; Howe and Eisenhart, 1990)—in the interest of gathering more kinds of information that would permit more comprehensive analyses of complicated processes like education (Gage, 1989; Taylor, 1989). Another way to think about collaboration among researchers is to consider interdisciplinary collaboration, i.e., the collaboration of educational psychologists with educational anthropologists, or with educational sociologists; the collaboration of educational anthropologists with political scientists or economists; the collaboration of disciplinary specialists with mathematics educators, science educators, or reading specialists. Interdisciplinary collaboration is the topic of this chapter.

We think that interdisciplinary collaboration holds special promise for research on classrooms because it addresses the multifaceted nature of teaching, learning, and learning to teach. As Chapters 3 and 4 illustrated, teaching and learning are both psychological and social processes. They encompass both cultural and cognitive content. Learning to teach includes both knowledge acquisition and socialization into a community. Yet, these aspects are usually isolated for the purposes of research and investigated separately. At least in theory, collaborative research projects involving psychologists and anthropologists should permit these aspects of classrooms to be studied together, thereby increasing the comprehensiveness and consequently the usefulness of the work.

However, despite its potential, interdisciplinary collaborative research has received little systematic attention in the educational research literature. For example, there seems to be only limited awareness that different assumptions underlie what is called "interdisciplinary collaboration" in educational research. Our reading of the literature indicates that there are at least two views of how different disciplines might be joined in the study of classrooms. One view is captured in Shulman's statement, "knowing well is knowing in more than a single way" (Shulman, 1988b, p. 23). Following Shulman, discipline-based research entails the application of disciplinary canons—such as those for formulating research questions, discovering information, and verifying its accuracy—to a topic of interest, e.g., education (Shulman, 1988a). A "field" such as education serves as a locus for discipline-based studies, in which researchers from various disciplines raise questions and pursue them in ways that are anchored by, and characteristic of, their respective disciplines [see also Eisenhart (1988)]. Although Shulman acknowledged that researchers who apply disciplinary tenets outside their original contexts may change the tenets in some ways, he argued that such changes ordinarily do not compromise the principles of the discipline. Thus,

As each of these disciplinary perspectives is brought to bear on the field of education, it brings with it its own set of concepts, methods, and procedures, often modifying them to fit the phenomena or problems of education. Such modifications, however, can rarely violate the principles defining those disciplines from which the methods were drawn (Shulman, 1988a, p. 5).

Our reading of Shulman suggests that in his view, to the extent that concepts and methods from disciplines differ, the achievement of shared purposes may not be either possible or desirable when it comes to interdisciplinary research. Rather, as he advised,

*. . . the most effective programs of educational research are likely to be charac-
terized by what Merton (1975), the distinguished sociologist, or Schwab
(1969), the eminent philosopher of education, have called applications of
"disciplined eclectic." The best research program will reflect intelligent
deployment of a diversity of research methods applied to their appropriate
research questions. (Shulman, 1988a, p. 16)*

To us, this view implies a form of collaboration that is additive or parallel in
nature, in which findings are considered side by side, rather than necessarily in an integrated fashion.

A second view relies on ideas from studies of small-group interactions,
sociolinguistic conventions, and dialogic processes [see, for example, Barnes
and Todd (1977); Edwards and Mercer (1987)]. These ideas are generally
consistent with both a Vygotskian social constructivist view, e.g., Tharp and
Gallimore (1988) and a critical pedagogy view, e.g., Habermas (1982), that
novel or creative analyses can emerge from carefully designed and mutually conducted social activities and talk (see also Bruner, 1986). Ideally,
social interactions facilitate open and frank discussions among persons with
different perspectives and commitments, and they result in the development of mutual or shared understandings. Shared understandings, which
in some sense reflect a more sophisticated and productive level of understanding than persons would probably achieve on their own, are the hallmark of this form of collaboration.

In addition to the educational research community's failure to recognize, at least explicitly, that these two views of interdisciplinary collaboration (and perhaps others) exist, we know of few systematic assessments of
the nature or amount of interdisciplinary collaboration that has actually
occurred in research projects about teaching or learning in classrooms. Few
researchers who have tried interdisciplinary collaboration explain later how
they did it or how well it worked.

As we have already indicated, we have been trying to produce some
form of collaboration in our own work together. When we started, we were
simply "working together" and, until we had completed one major study
together, we never considered explicitly what kind of collaboration we had
or how it fit with the literature's descriptions. After embarking on a second
major study together and as this book nears completion, we still have many
questions about the process of collaboration and about the ultimate outcomes of our collaborative efforts.

In our Learning to Teach Mathematics study, our attempts to develop a
more integrated form of collaboration have been on-going. As described
earlier, when we first decided to prepare a response to the Request For Proposals about mathematics and science education issued by the National
Science Foundation, the two of us and the mathematics educators on our

team agreed to focus on changes in the student teachers' knowledge, beliefs, and thinking, and on the social contexts in which they learned to teach. This direction seemed productive because, at a general level at least, it covered areas in which all of us were interested.[1]

When we began to develop a list of research questions for our study, we followed the same pattern of aggregating our interests that we had used in our earlier study of the acquisition of reading. Each researcher created a list of research questions derived from her or his background knowledge. As a team we discussed the questions and then added them together into one list.

For example, Borko's questions focused on individual novice teachers and changes in their knowledge and thinking during their final year of teacher preparation and their first year of teaching. The project's attention to these questions is reflected in the following subset of the original research questions (Jones, Agard, Borko, Brown, Eisenhart, and Underhill, 1989):

1. What content, pedagogical, and pedagogical content knowledge do participants in this study have? How does the knowledge of participants change over time?

2. What is the nature of the participants' thinking during preactive, interactive, and postactive teaching? How does the thinking of participants change over time?

3. What is the relationship between participants' thinking and their knowledge?

In contrast, Eisenhart was interested in the cultures of teaching and the social organization of mathematics teaching in two kinds of settings—the university teacher education program and the public schools—where the novices were learning to become mathematics teachers. Her interests were reflected in another subset of the original research questions:

1. What are the cultures of teaching in the university setting?

2. What is the social organization of learning to teach mathematics in the university setting?

3. What are the cultures of teaching in the public schools where the novices completed their student teaching and their first year of teaching?

4. What is the social organization of learning to teach mathematics in the public school settings?

As these lists illustrate, we used our individual interests in the initial design of our study of learning to teach mathematics.[2] However, we found ourselves without much sense of how to build a conceptual framework that, following Shulman, would incorporate perspectives from the disciplines of cognitive psychology and anthropology without compromising the principles of either discipline; nor for how to reach the shared understanding envisioned by Barnes, Todd, Edwards, and Mercer. We realized that we needed to give our collaboration more thought.

ANOTHER ATTEMPT TO COLLABORATE

In the summer of 1989—after the completion of data collection for Year 1 of the project and following a partial review of the classroom research conducted from the perspectives of cognitive psychology and educational anthropology—we again met as a group, this time to formulate a design for analyses of the data. At this point, our commitment to collaboration was put to a new and more crucial test. Unlike the earlier investigation of reading, we were determined that our analyses would incorporate the perspectives of our full project team. We wanted to learn from the expertise of each other and to develop an analysis plan that would more truly integrate our different perspectives.

At this point we were also better prepared to collaborate. Our clarification of the major themes that each discipline brings to the study of classrooms gave us guides to use to check that our investigation of becoming a mathematics teacher was accommodating both psychological and anthropological perspectives. With this knowledge and increased motivation we again tackled the collaboration issue in our research.

After extensive discussions and an initial reading of a sample of the data, we developed a conceptual model to guide our data analysis. The original model has been slightly revised for our purposes here (see Figure 1 for the revised version). As Figure 1 depicts, our ultimate goal was to describe and explain changes in the novice teachers' knowledge, thinking, and actions related to the teaching of mathematics over the two-year course of our study (Box 1). Prior goals were to describe and explain the contexts for learning to teach created by the intersection of the novice teachers' knowledge, thinking, and actions in the classroom at selected points in time (Box 2); their university teacher education experiences (Box 3); and their experiences in the public schools where they student taught (in Year 1) and held their first full-time teaching positions (in Year 2; Box 4). Together these contexts were assumed to be the primary constituents of what the novice teachers learned. Secondary sources of influences were expected to be their prior experiences (Box 5) and the research project itself (Box 6). In what follows, we discuss Boxes 1 through 4.

The revised conceptual model committed us (Eisenhart and Borko) to a specific relationship between our original two sets of research questions.

FIGURE 5-1

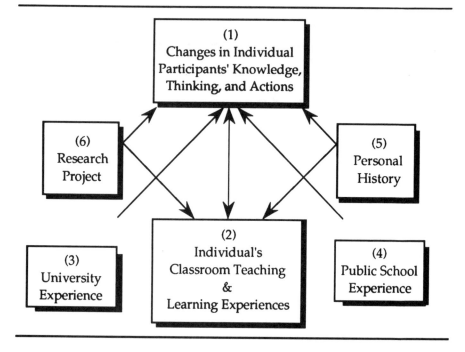

First, we committed ourselves to a focus on the individual who was learning to teach and to the relationships among her knowledge, thinking, and actions as she learned to teach. To both of us, the focus on the individual seemed reasonable; neither anthropologist nor psychologist could dispute that it is the individual who learns. For Eisenhart the attention to individual mental and behavioral processes was a turn away from the group processes and identity formation she was concentrating on in her other work (Eisenhart, 1990). Had she designed this study alone, she probably would have chosen to focus on the novice teachers' formation of social and personal identities in the context of their peer groups. In a sense then, she risked her personal scholarship agenda to pursue the collaboration. However, because she was trained (for the most part) in the tradition of cognitive anthropology and inspired by the work of cognitive anthropologists Roy D'Andrade, Michael Cole, Jean Lave, and Dorothy Holland, it was not heretical to focus on cognitive processes. In fact, this focus is consistent with what researchers in the subfield have been encouraging for some time. For example, Cole and Scribner wrote, "we believe that unless there is some agreement on what 'cognitive consequences' we are studying, there are no guidelines for deciding what aspects of culture are relevant to the search for 'critical socializing' experiences" (Cole and

Scribner, 1976, pp. 159–160). Given this and the nature of our second commitment, the central place of cognitive processes seemed justified.

Our second commitment was to the position that the primary source and direction of influence on changes over time in the individual novice teacher's knowledge and behavior was the sociocultural environment created by the public schools, the university teacher education program, and her own immediate experiences (or responses) in classrooms (both as student and teacher). In this case, Borko had to gamble. Had she designed the study alone, she probably would have focused almost exclusively on the individual novice teachers, seeking to identify patterns of change in their knowledge, thinking, and actions, and to relate these patterns to a model of the development of pedagogical expertise (Berliner, 1989). However, to her, the decision to examine sociocultural influences on individuals' changes did not seem to compromise the principles of cognitive psychology. On the contrary, it seemed to offer the potential for a richer understanding of the complex process of cognitive growth. Further, Borko found support for this broader view of cognition within the ranks of cognitive psychology. As Putnam, Lampert, and Peterson noted, there is "a growing movement within cognitive science to question the fundamental view of thinking and knowing underlying current cognitive theories. Rather than viewing knowledge and thinking as existing within the mind of the individual, cognition is considered to be interactively situated in physical and social contexts" (Putnam, et al., 1990, p.68).

Despite the commitments entailed in the model, we began with analyses of separate components of the model, in order to take advantage of our respective methodological strengths. Borko's first task was to develop case studies of each participant's knowledge, thinking, and actions, applying the cognitive psychologist's lens. Eisenhart's first task was to develop a picture of the university teacher education experience, using her anthropologist's lens. Borko's work first produced cases for two (of the eight) student teachers ("Ms. Daniels" and "Ms. Jenkins") who were closely followed in the study, and Eisenhart's work first produced a preliminary analysis of the messages conveyed by and the social organization of the university teacher education program in which the student teachers were enrolled (Eisenhart, Behm, and Romagnano, 1991).

With these analyses to consider, we realized that we had again put off the question of exactly how we would integrate them. Placing them side-by-side in an article or final report would merely include them both; we would still have only additive or parallel collaboration. We decided to try the approach of picking critical incidents or events as loci for bringing both analyses to bear. We reasoned that by asking ourselves to provide *an* explanation for *an* incident (and over time accumulating such explanations), we would force ourselves to deal squarely with the intersections and discrepancies between our approaches.

We chose as our first incident an occasion when Ms. Daniels tried to explain division of fractions to a sixth-grade class in which she was the student teacher. In what follows, we briefly describe the incident as Borko interpreted it, as Eisenhart related data from the university program to it, and our joint analysis of it, in order to illustrate the type of collaboration in which we are now engaged.[3]

A CRITICAL INCIDENT OF CLASSROOM TEACHING

The setting was a whole-class review lesson on division of fractions designed to help prepare Ms. Daniels' students for the standardized test: Survey of Basic Skills. Ms. Daniels planned to focus on procedural understanding and she began the lesson by reviewing the algorithm for division of fractions. In response to a student's (Elise) question about why you invert and multiply, Ms. Daniels attempted to provide a concrete example (having one-half of the paint needed to paint the remaining three-fourths of a fence and computing what fraction of the fence would remain unpainted) and accompanying diagram. She realized part way through the example that it illustrated multiplication rather than division. She abandoned the example and, for the remainder of the lesson, demonstrated use of the algorithm and helped the students to practice it. In discussing the incident later that day, Ms. Daniels stated that "the explanation . . . wasn't very good. But I think by the end of the time, that they had picked up on it." Because the students seemed able to apply the algorithm correctly, she was pleased with the lesson. After the lesson, Ms. Daniels' major concern was that it had taken too much time.

The Psychologist's Case

Borko's analysis was based on daily observations of Ms. Daniels teaching mathematics and interviews with her about the lessons during three one-week data-collection cycles at the beginning, middle, and end of her student teaching year. Borko found that this incident illustrates several issues that were evident in Ms. Daniels' pedagogical thinking and actions throughout the year: the tension between teaching for conceptual versus procedural knowledge, the importance of practice, the desire to use concrete and semiconcrete (visual) representations, and the need for time management. For Ms. Daniels, one of the most salient dilemmas about teaching appeared to be the relative emphasis to place on conceptual versus procedural knowledge. Throughout the year, the value she placed on learning algorithms and procedural skills, and on practicing them until they are "engraved in your brain," is clear. The majority of lessons we observed reflected this value. They consisted of homework check, demonstration of an algorithm, and guided and independent practice of the algorithm. However, also clear in the observations of Ms. Daniels and interviews about her teaching is a concern that students acquire a conceptual knowledge of mathematics, that they learn "why as well as how mathematics works." She attempted to teach for conceptual knowledge, to some extent, in each of her student teaching placements. Some of these attempts were successful; others were not.

Six dimensions seemed to distinguish lessons when Ms. Daniels met her goal of teaching for conceptual understanding from those when she did not. The first dimension was Ms. Daniels' conceptual understanding of the topic (was it strong or weak?). The additional dimensions included: Ms. Daniels' ability to think of concrete or visual representations (did one come to mind immediately or not?); her perception of her students' ability levels (were they strong or weak in math?); her perception of her cooperating teachers' priorities (did they emphasize conceptual understanding or learning of algorithms and procedures?); her classification of the lesson type (e.g., was it introduction, practice, or review?); and finally, her own priorities for the class (how important were issues such as classroom management and curriculum coverage?).

Thus, Borko's explanation of the focal incident took the following form. Ms. Daniels' knowledge of division of fractions was apparently weak. (This inference is corroborated by additional interviews in which her ability to work problems involving division of fractions and to explain them was examined.) When Ms. Daniels tried to answer Elise's question, she immediately thought of a real-life application and accompanying representation, as was her stated preference. But as she began to solve the application problem, she realized that she had created a representation for multiplication of fractions rather than division. Further, she was unable to think quickly of an appropriate representation for division. Then, because Ms. Daniels classified the lesson as a review, perceived her students as in need of practice with algorithms in order to do well on the upcoming test, thought her time for the review was limited, and believed her cooperating teacher's priority was to give the students what they needed for the test, she decided to abandon the attempt to provide a conceptual explanation for Elise's question and to focus instead on procedural understanding. Given this decision-making process, Ms. Daniels was able to conclude that the lesson had gone fairly well.

Borko's analysis reflects several of the themes in cognitive psychological research on classrooms. Its primary focus is on the individual student teacher—Ms. Daniels—and the relationships among her knowledge, thinking, and actions. It argues that Ms. Daniels' classroom actions (her demonstration of the algorithm for division of fractions and provision of guided practice) are at least partially determined by her knowledge system (weak content knowledge of division of fractions, inadequate pedagogical content knowledge of powerful explanations and examples) and her pedagogical reasoning (inability to think of an appropriate representation). These factors affect her decisions (the interactive decision to abandon the attempt to provide a conceptual explanation for division of fractions) and, ultimately, her actions in the classroom.

The Anthropologist's Portrayal of External Influences

Analysis of data obtained about the mathematics methods course and the teacher education program that Ms. Daniels was enrolled in during her student teaching year revealed a striking resemblance between Ms. Daniels' experience in her own classroom and what had happened five months earlier in the mathematics methods course she took at the university. In the course, the student teachers had the same question that troubled Elise, and the instructor's conscientious attempts to provide a conceptual explanation of division of fractions and to demonstrate it with a manipulative failed to clear up their confusion.

Based on observations of the mathematics methods course and interviews with the student teachers and instructor about the course and the teacher education program, Ms. Daniels' approach in her own classroom reflected a recurrent theme in both the mathematics methods course and the student teachers' overall responses to their teacher education coursework. In the mathematics methods course, concrete examples were stressed as tools to facilitate conceptual explanations and understandings; as part of a routine they practiced repeatedly in the course, the student teachers learned to begin each lesson on a new topic with an application or example. Also in the methods course, relatively little attention was given to commonsense verbal explanations of mathematical operations or procedures. Thus, the student teachers learned to expect that the route to conceptual understanding in mathematics passed necessarily through concrete examples illustrating that the standard algorithm produced the correct answer. This is the same route that Ms. Daniels took in the division of fractions review lesson.

Further, in the teacher education program as a whole, Ms. Daniels and the other student teachers found themselves in a context where activities that could be directly imported to their classrooms for a particular lesson became more important for them to learn than verbal, theoretical, or abstract explanations of the information covered in the lesson (Eisenhart et al., 1991). We think that this preference for what the student teachers called "ideas that will work" was created by the multiple demands placed on the student teachers by the teacher education program. For example, the university required that student teachers give time and energy to being good university students (their grades in coursework and student teaching were important to them and their futures), good teachers, and "professionals" in a wide range of areas from dress to speech to punctuality, and to making schoolwork into such things as "conceptual" experiences for students. At the same time, cooperating teachers required these student teachers to be good disciplinarians, cover specified material, and help out with numerous odd jobs. Added to all this, the student teachers themselves wanted to "motivate" their students, "make learning fun," and be seen by others, especially their cooperating teachers and university supervisors, as competent, or at least promising, teachers. In this tangle of competing expectations, the student teachers were asked to find their own way, to take responsibility for their lives, to solve their own problems, to make their own decisions, to plan their own lessons, and to innovate as much as possible.

Given the competing demands that the student teachers faced in the program and the fact that they had to student teach during at least some portion of every school day, they simply did not have the time to carefully construct and reflect upon their own set of classroom activities, routines, and strategies for each lesson they were called upon to teach. Instead, they tried to piece together classroom activities—activities they could use, often the very next day—from the ideas they got from their university professors and supervisors, cooperating teachers, and peers. This also appears to be the route Ms. Daniels took in her own classroom. When called upon to answer Elise's question, Ms. Daniels instantly tried to recall an example that her mathematics methods instructor had used to "explain" fractions and began to apply it in her classroom. Unfortunately, her knowledge base, created in part by her experiences in the mathematics methods course and her peers' collective response to what they should be learning in their methods courses, was extremely thin, and she ran into problems with the example she recalled.

Thus, Eisenhart's analysis focuses on the competing cultural (or normative) messages given and received about teaching and learning mathematics in the context of a particular methods course and teacher education program. It reveals some of the ways in which cultural messages and features of the social organization of learning-to-teach environments create the conditions in which student teachers learn, as well as the conditions of *what* they learn. Although incomplete as an anthropological analysis (because we have not yet included various actors' responses to the conditions nor their distinct voices), we think the stage has been set for making connections from the methods course and the program to wider traditions of teacher education and mathematics education. For example, the course instructor's modeling of routines and his emphasis on conceptual understanding may connect to two distinct traditions of mathematics education: behaviorist and cognitivist teaching. Similarly, the various demands placed on the student teachers may connect to divergent societal expectations that teachers be both socializers and academicians. We think these linkages and their implications for what student teachers and teacher educators think and do in their classrooms can be revealed as we pursue our present collaborative course.

A Preliminary Integration

Looking at both sets of preliminary findings and bringing to bear our disciplinary frameworks, we are beginning to see the outlines of a more unified understanding of the learning to teach process we have been studying —an understanding that acknowledges the complex interplay of individual novice teachers' characteristics and messages from the university and public school environments. For example, we think that the critical incident involving Ms. Daniels' attempt to teach division of fractions reveals dilemmas that play themselves out throughout the data we have analyzed so far. An example is the dilemma between teaching for procedural versus conceptual knowledge. The procedural "horn" is represented in the mostly implicit belief, held by the student teachers and cooperating teachers, that mathematical learning occurs bit-by-bit through the accumulation of procedural routines and practice. It is also represented in the curriculum directives and norms of the schools we studied, as well as in some parts of the teacher education program. The conceptual horn is represented by more explicitly held beliefs in constructivism, experiential and group activities, and life-long learning, emphasized (somewhat ambivalently) by the university and the mathematics education community. Student teachers are caught squarely between the horns: they are held accountable by the placement schools and their own beliefs to focus on procedural aspects. At the same time, they are asked to accept and demonstrate the university's priorities as conditions of successfully completing the teacher education program and joining the professional community. The dilemma is compounded by the reality of time constraints. Because mathematics is allocated only a certain amount of time in the school day, it is often not possible to achieve both sets of goals. It is further compounded by limitations in the student teachers' conceptual understanding of mathematics. Although they expressed commitment to the idea of conceptual understanding they were frustrated in their own learning experiences and fearful of what would happen in their own classroom. The division of fractions incident is illustrative of the student teachers' responses to these dilemmas. Given the reality of conflicting priorities and expectations, time constraints, and her own

fragile knowledge system, Ms. Daniels' abandonment of the visual representation and retreat to a procedurally-focused lesson is not surprising. In
general, dilemmas such as this led the student teachers to paths of least
resistance, "quick fix" solutions for the competing demands they faced, and
confusion about professional knowledge and identity.

CONCLUSIONS

In conclusion, we now have evidence that the ways of thinking and acting
that unfold in our participants as they become teachers are not constructed
by them alone; rather they appear to be the products—some intended and
some unintended—of the interaction between our participants' knowledge
and actions and a teacher education program whose parts are multifaceted
and loosely coupled and whose normative agenda is complicated and far-
reaching. Had we chosen to look at only one facet of the program—say, the
student teachers' planning or their interactive decisions—and proceeded to
draw conclusions or make recommendations based on those data, we
would have missed much of what makes up and constrains the ideas and
actions of student teachers as they are preparing to teach. Had we chosen to
look at the teacher education program without participants' responses to it,
we would not have seen how participants' own actions and ideas contribute
to what is being learned.

To the extent that we eventually succeed in identifying and coming to
understand the interconnections and contributions of the various factors
that make up learning to teach as it occurred in our study, we will attribute
our success to our interdisciplinary collaboration and to our decision to
focus on critical incidents. If we were gamblers, we would bet now on our
ability to keep our disciplinary orientations clearly and distinctly in front of
us, so that one focus is not subsumed by the other, and so that our data may
be assessed from both standpoints and then integrated. The focus on critical
incidents has facilitated our efforts. Attempting to understand the interplay
of multiple factors in a learning-to-teach process that spans two years
proved initially to be an overwhelming task. By directing our attention to
single incidents, one at a time, we think that we can produce a comprehensive and coherent account of what an individual demonstrates she knows
and is able to do in the context of what she has been exposed to within a
teacher education program.

As we continue to develop interconnected analyses of various critical
incidents from the standpoint of anthropologist and psychologist and to
accumulate them along with the analyses of mathematics knowledge provided by the mathematics educators on our team, we are optimistic that the
patterns that emerge will provide new and important insights about the

process of learning to teach—insights with implications for the improvement of teacher education programs. For example, we think that the conflicting messages, highlighted in our study by virtue of our interdisciplinary approach, are commonplace in American teacher education programs today and are likely to become somewhat worse. Certainly in the fields of mathematics education and literacy education, which (at least in the United States) are undergoing wholesale changes in perspective (e.g., to constructivist teaching; to whole language instruction), competing messages within teacher education programs of the near future seem inevitable, unless some steps are taken quickly. As teacher educators adopt new perspectives, they also are likely to hold on to some of their old ways. They must struggle with the new and the old, and out of such struggles is likely to come confusion in their presentations and advice to novice teachers. Teacher educators and prospective teachers also will continue to confront the competing influences and demands of the public schools. Our analysis of even a single incident reveals the complex interplay of cognitive and cultural influences on learning to teach and the multiple, sometimes conflicting messages given by the various sources of influence. We think that the conflicting messages received by the student teachers in Ms. Daniels' program limited the program's effectiveness in achieving its goal of helping novice teachers to learn to teach for conceptual understanding. Further, we think that the program could be modified to eliminate some of the conflict (e.g., by selecting public school placements that are more compatible with the goals of the university program; by redesigning the mathematics methods course so that models of teaching for conceptual understanding are more consistently presented), making the professional socialization of teachers a smoother process, and enabling them to acquire more easily the knowledge and the commitment needed to teach for conceptual understanding. Such steps will not be easy; however, we think that analyses such as ours permit teacher educators to pinpoint what the conflicting pressures are and thus to face, with a clearer and more comprehensive view, the tough decisions that must be made and the priorities that must be established in the redesign of a teacher education program.

Finally, to return to our more general discussion of interdisciplinary collaborative research and to comment on where we stand, we now think that the separate questions, data-collection plans, and analysis schemes we retained for so long in our work together reflect Shulman's call to deploy "a diversity of research methods . . . to know well . . . in more than a single way." However, this approach seems to be, at its roots, an additive or parallel form of collaboration. The work we are now doing as we attempt to explain cases like Ms. Daniels' through salient critical incidents seems to represent a more integrative collaboration in which we are moving closer to shared and more productive understandings. As we continue to interact, we find that we have grown closer to sharing the same knowledge in at least some senses; that is, Eisenhart knows what Borko means when she asks group members to construct case studies of novice teachers' classroom teaching. Her intention is to figure out how all the potential sources of influence we studied (prior beliefs, competence in mathematics, experiences in the public school, instruction in the mathematics methods course, etc.) affected the teachers' thinking and actions in the classroom. Borko's ultimate aim is to label and characterize the strategies (both cognitive and behavioral) that novice teachers learn to use in their classrooms. Having no unassailable access to those strategies, she hopes to build a case for her assertions from the convergence of explicitly stated strategies (as in interviews) and those inferred from the analyses of social contexts.

By the same token, Borko knows what Eisenhart means when she asks the group to consider how situational constraints emerging from the juxta-position of competing demands from the teacher education program and the public school settings repeatedly create the conditions for student teachers to come up with "quick fix" solutions—solutions considered undesirable especially by teacher educators. Her ultimate aim is to map the social arrangements and ideological orientations that characterize the whole teacher education experience. Also lacking unassailable evidence, she intends to build her case from evidence of recurrent patterns that produce dilemmas that must be solved in some way by the student teachers as they take action in their learning-to-teach worlds.

However, sharing this knowledge is not the same thing as Eisenhart agreeing that elucidation of individual cognition should be the highest or single priority of this research project; or Borko agreeing that the characterization of the teacher education experience should be primary. Were either to agree, she would seem to be compromising her disciplinary commitment. What we have achieved, and what seems to us to be an important step toward more integrative collaboration, is a set of tentative commitments through relatively minor compromise. Although we can imagine that the search for principles that will transcend our fundamentally different views of the world could be fruitful and is certainly a laudable pursuit, we are not there yet.

NOTES

1. In this book we will discuss primarily the contributions of educational anthropology and cognitive psychology to our study of learning to teach mathematics. As anthropologist and psychologist working together, the two of us have struggled most with how to describe and relate our disciplinary perspectives in order to produce an explicit conceptual framework for studying *how* individuals

learn to become mathematics teachers. The mathematics education researchers on our team also make crucial contributions from the perspective of their field. These contributions focus attention on *what* (the content that) is being learned as well as how it is being learned. [For examples of our initial steps to integrate their strengths, see Borko, Eisenhart, Brown, Underhill, Jones and Agard (1992), and Eisenhart, Borko, Underhill, Brown, Jones and Agard (in press)].

2. [For detailed descriptions of the methodology used and the characteristics of individuals selected to participate in this study, see Jones et al. (1989) and Borko, Brown, Underhill, Eisenhart, Jones and Agard (1990)]. We have not included details of our methodology here because they are not necessary to illustrate the way in which the project represents our collaborative efforts.

3. What follows is not a complete account of the incident. It illustrates only a portion of the psychological and anthropological themes we are developing. More complete analyses appear in Borko et al., (1992) and Eisenhart et al., (in press).

► **6**

Using Classroom
Research in Classroom
Practice

With this chapter we begin a two-part discussion of a different and difficult issue: the standards that should be applied to the conduct of classroom research. In our minds, this issue has two main parts. First, we think that classroom research should be held to a standard of usefulness and value to educational practitioners, policy-makers, and concerned citizens. In addition, we expect classroom research to meet standards of accepted theoretical and methodological practice as defined by the educational research community. Addressing both parts of this issue simultaneously, as they need to be, is not a simple matter. In this chapter, we focus on the first part, how to conduct classroom research that will be useful and valuable to classroom practice. In Chapter 7, we take up the second part, the standards we need to meet if our research is to be considered credible within the educational research community. And, we try to incorporate both parts into an overall set of standards of validity for classroom research.

It is painfully obvious that much classroom research never finds its way into schools or classrooms, at least not as the researchers intended. Why has the translation of classroom research findings into practice been so limited? Why does research not inform more directly the practices of those most involved in public education, e.g., teachers, principals, parents? These are troubling questions for educational researchers and policy-makers, and ones that have come up over and over again in research reports and reform agenda of the past decade.

We see two related sets of issues as central to attempts to improve the research-practice connection. The first has to do with the nature of the research enterprise. For classroom research to be useful and valuable, educational researchers must ask questions of relevance and importance to practitioners and policy-makers, and they must design research programs that take into account the characteristics of classroom life as practitioners know them. The second set of issues relates to patterns of communication among researchers, practitioners, and policy-makers. For classroom research to have an impact on educational practice, findings must be made accessible to practitioners in a timely fashion and in a form that can be understood and translated into action.

The second set of issues, insofar as it focuses on conditions outside of the actual research process, is beyond the scope of this book. However, we briefly mention a number of sources to which the reader can turn for additional information. Many useful ideas can be found in the literature on change. Some theorists (Sarason, 1971) argue that research results will not be implemented unless certain conditions conducive to the change are already in place in schools and classrooms. For example, it is commonplace to read that research results will find their way into practice when the results make sense in terms of what educators already believe or are concerned about (Eisenhart, Shrum, Cuthbert, and Harding, 1987; Hall and Loucks, 1978; in Lampert, 1988), when rewards within a school can be made to support a practice or change consistent with research results (Glickman, 1985; Lampert, 1988), or when teachers can be made aware of how their own beliefs conflict with empirical evidence from research studies (Fenstermacher, 1986; V. Richardson, Casanova, Placier, and Guilfoyle, 1989; Richardson-Koehler and Fenstermacher, 1988).

Research on the dissemination and utilization of scientific knowledge (Huberman, 1990) is also relevant. This literature suggests that a major determinant of whether research results find their way into practitioner organizations is "the number, variety, and mutuality of contacts between researchers and practitioners, i.e., . . . their degree of interrelatedness" (Huberman, 1990, p. 364). In line with this suggestion, organizations such as the National Education Association are experimenting with computer networks to facilitate dialogue between researchers and practitioners that is designed specifically to facilitate the application of research findings to problems raised by practitioners in their daily lives.

The first set of issues, on the other hand, clearly falls within the purview of this book. It encompasses topics such as the identification of research problems, the design of research programs, and appropriate roles for teachers and researchers in the research enterprise. These topics, and other questions related to the design and conduct of classroom research, are the major issues addressed in this chapter.

IMPEDIMENTS TO USEFUL AND
VALUABLE CLASSROOM RESEARCH

A number of factors seem to work against the design and conduct of class-room research that is potentially useful and valuable to practitioners and policy-makers. First, there is the reality of differences in the social organiza-tion of teachers' versus researchers' work. Differences in the two groups' work underlie and serve to maintain different beliefs, concerns, and values. Differences in the two groups' responsibilities on the job, in the kinds of rewards available to each group for a job well done, and in ways of talking about what is significant or important and why, create conditions in which teachers and researchers have trouble communicating meaningfully with each other or establishing shared purposes. These conditions set the stage for differences in the way problems in classroom practice are identified and in the way solutions are proposed and implemented [see also Florio-Ruane (1990), Florio-Ruane and Dohanich (1984), Lampert (1985), for other discus-sions of the "two communities" problem].

Conventionally educational researchers approach the definition of problems to study in terms of existing scholarly literature. Scholarly tradi-tions are, by their very nature, analytic; that is, parts of complex phenom-ena, such as the lived reality of classrooms, are identified, separated, cate-gorized, and isolated for specific investigation. This is particularly true of experimental, correlational, or survey designs that emphasize the use of standardized measures permitting consistency of observations across sites, the manipulation of controls, and the determination of statistically signifi-cant differences among groups. Over time, these procedures have been codified into sets of technical routines, some of which are difficult for lay-persons to follow, that encourage the aggregation of data from many differ-ent sites and, subsequently, the eclipse of site-specific information. Even when naturalistic, ethnographic, or case study designs are used—designs intended to recognize or preserve complexity, researchers simplify settings by making decisions about what topics are most important to pursue, what kinds of data are most important to gather, what categories of information are most important to analyze, and what themes are most important to elaborate.

In contrast, classroom teachers tend to pose problems in terms of very specific and immediate situations, e.g., "Why isn't Jimmy learning to read as fast as he should?" "What can I do about the five students who can't keep up with the class?" "How do I prepare my class for standardized tests without 'teaching to the test?'" "How do I keep from making a token out of my one black student?" Their orientation can be characterized as synthetic; that is, an attempt to bring many ideas together to address a particular classroom situation. Further, unlike researchers, classroom teachers are regularly confronted with incommensurable problems, such as how to manage the class, how to convey mathematics, and how to assure gender equity (Lampert, 1985), *and* the need to act immediately in the course of classroom activity. They must decide what to do on-the-spot, and as Lampert suggested, perhaps the best they can hope for is to pursue the least harmful alternative, all things considered. Lampert wrote:

> *When I consider the conflicts that arise in the classroom from my perspective as a teacher, I do not see a choice between abstract social goals, such as Excellence versus Equality or Freedom versus Standardization. What I see are tensions between individual students, or personal confrontations between myself and a particular group of boys or girls. When I think about rewarding Dennis's excellent, though boisterous, contributions to problem-solving discussion, while at the same time encouraging reticent Sandra to take an equal part in class activities, I cannot see my goals as a neat dichotomy and my job as making clear choices. My aims for any one particular student are tangled with my aims for each of the others in the class, and, more importantly, I am responsible for choosing a course of action in circumstances where choice leads to further conflict. (Lampert, 1985, pp. 181–182)*

When teachers attempt to solve classroom problems, they usually must make adjustments quickly, without time for careful consideration and study, and get on with trying to produce the best teaching outcomes possible. And, they do not find it easy to think about answers or solutions, much less try them out, separate from the demands and complexity of their own classrooms and occupational requirements. Lampert captured the differences in solution strategies of teachers and researchers well when she wrote:

> *As the teacher considers alternative solutions to any particular problem, she cannot hope to arrive at the "right" alternative in the sense that a theory built on valid and reliable empirical data can be said to be right. This is because she brings many contradictory aims to each instance of her work, and the resolution of their dissonance cannot be neat or simple. Even though she cannot find their right solutions, however, the teacher must do something about the problems she faces. (Lampert, 1985, p. 181)*

Teachers cannot afford the time to meet strict standards of academic research design, nor are they rewarded for doing so. Researchers, on the other hand, *must* meet these standards if their work is to be viewed positively by their academic peers, and in so doing, they cannot respond fast enough to help teachers when they most need help. Further, in meeting the conditions for good academic research, researchers may alter the problem and its solution beyond recognition by teachers.

Another problem, also related to the identification of research questions, stems from the fact that researchers often ignore the specific and local characteristics of classrooms when defining problems and designing research studies. As we noted in Chapter 2, Doyle identified a number of properties of classroom settings that create pressures that shape the task of teaching: multidimensionality, simultaneity, immediacy, unpredictability, publicness, and history (Doyle, 1986). When these properties and the pressures they create are simplified or ignored by educational researchers, it is unlikely that research findings will address the concerns of practitioners or be easily translatable into classroom actions. What is more likely is the situation often reported by teachers—that the research available to them lacks practicality and is inconsistent with classroom reality. In other words, "teachers frequently are given answers to questions they never asked and solutions to problems they never had" (Tikunoff and Ward, 1983, p. 454; see also Oja and Smulyan, 1989).

A third problem relates to differences in intended uses for research findings. Researchers see the significance of research in terms of its implications for understanding far-ranging repercussions, predicting and improving the future, informing policy, or getting tenure, whereas teachers usually want research results to bear directly on their classroom practice. Their approaches to the long-term problems identified by researchers as associated with the practice of tracking in secondary schools (Oakes, 1985) are illustrative. For teachers, the day-to-day instructional difficulties that result from not tracking appear to outweigh the long-term dangers. Because they find it much easier to teach homogeneously grouped children, the findings from research tend to be of little compelling interest. In contrast, for researchers who do not, in the course of their research, face students everyday, the short-term gains of tracking do not outweigh the dangers of repeated use of this strategy.

BEYOND THE "GREAT DIVIDE": TEACHER-RESEARCHER COLLABORATION

These differences in teachers' and researchers' work and their orientations to the research enterprise suggest that, before research results will find their way into teaching practice, some ways must be found to bridge the gap between teachers and researchers. Many researchers and policy-makers have struggled with the question of how to bridge that gap. One strategy that has frequently been proposed is a more active involvement by teachers in the research enterprise. Suggested models for increased teacher involvement, although they vary greatly, are often grouped together under the umbrella of "teacher-researcher collaboration." At one extreme, researchers have involved teachers in a fairly minimal way by seeking their input about characteristics of classes or students that should be taken into account during the data-collection process. For example, in the Learning to Teach Mathematics research project, we asked novice teachers, before each observed class session, what their goals were for the lesson, what activities were planned, and if there were specific aspects of the class session to which we should pay particular attention. Our observation guidelines were developed to take into account that input (Jones et al., 1989).

At the other extreme are models calling for teachers to be fully engaged in every step of the research project. In one model of research at this end of the continuum, teachers and researchers work together to set common goals, mutually plan the research design, collect and analyze data, and interpret and report results. Examples of this form of collaborative action research include the Interactive Research and Development on Teaching Study (Tikunoff, Ward and Griffin, 1979) and the Interactive Research and Development on Schooling Study (Griffin, Lieberman and Jacullo-Noto, 1983). In another model, teachers conduct their own independent "teacher-as-researcher" projects [see the literature on teacher as researcher, including, for example, Elliott (1990), Hitchcock and Hughes (1989), Hopkins (1985), and Kemmis (1982)]. As these models of action research have grown in popularity in the United States, United Kingdom, and Australia, researchers have begun to study the process itself, to examine what happens when teachers and university researchers come together to identify and work on problems of practice (Oja and Smulyan, 1989; Sirotnik and Goodlad, 1988).

Representing a more moderate position, some researchers have suggested that dialogue and negotiation among equal partners should be the model for teacher-researcher collaborations (Florio-Ruane, 1989; Oakes, Hare and Sirotnik, 1986). While acknowledging that the conventional relationship between researchers and teachers is asymmetrical and that the asymmetry is continually reinforced in the points of contact between institutions, groups, and individuals, proponents of equal partnerships think the potential benefits are worth the struggle to overcome convention. The basis for their position can be found in the desire to treat all stakeholders fairly and to involve teachers, in particular, in matters that affect them directly.

Others have suggested that teachers or the public name the problems in need of study, with researchers offering their expertise as a service to help teachers and communities answer the questions that puzzle them (Freedman, 1990; Scriven, 1986). The assumption here seems to be that teachers are in the better position to know what their problems are while researchers are in a better position to conduct investigations of problems. Still others have proposed that researchers should encourage teachers to make schools better by advising them of the results of research and the latest thinking within the scholarly community (Fenstermacher, 1986; V. Richardson and Anders, 1990). Here the assumption is that researchers have access to and time to synthesize the best information about how schools and classrooms should be run, and thus they are in a good position to encourage and channel the reform efforts of teachers.

Regardless of the particular model being proposed, the idea of increased teacher involvement in the research enterprise has become increasingly popular among both researchers and policy-makers. For example, teacher-researcher collaborations have been widely encouraged as a way to support innovation, creativity, and courageousness in schools (Holmes Group, 1990), the empowerment of teachers (V. Richardson and Anders, 1990), and the professionalization of teaching (Schlechty and Whitford, 1988). And, there is evidence to suggest that teacher-researcher collaborations can produce some desirable changes in classrooms and schools (Florio-Ruane, 1990; V. Richardson and Anders, 1990; Sirotnik and Goodlad, 1988) and can increase the likelihood that the results of research will be used in practice (Huberman, 1990).

In this chapter, we do not attempt to provide a systematic review of the literature on teacher-researcher collaboration. Nor do we attempt to categorize or otherwise make sense of the multiple meanings attributed to the concept. Our discussion has a much more narrow focus. We explore various ways in which teachers can become more involved in the research enterprise, and communication between teachers and researchers can be improved, to help increase the probability that classroom research will meet a standard of usefulness and value to educational practitioners, policy-makers, and concerned citizens. We also explore ways in which researchers can become more sensitive to classrooms and teachers, and can draw upon the expertise of teachers, in order to meet the standard.

ROLES FOR TEACHERS AND RESEARCHERS IN THE RESEARCH ENTERPRISE

In this section, we present our ideas about appropriate roles for teachers and researchers in the research enterprise. Because these roles may vary depending upon the step in the research process and type of research project, we separately address three topics: identifying research problems, conducting descriptive research, and conducting intervention research. Because we ourselves have not previously contributed to work in the area of teacher-researcher collaboration, our views represent a synthesis drawn from our reading of the literature, reviews by other scholars (Sirotnik, 1988; Tikunoff and Ward, 1983), and our own experience in interdisciplinary collaboration.

Identifying Research Problems

To ensure that classroom research is useful and valuable to practitioners, the problems to be studied must focus on the concerns of the research consumer—in this case, the classroom teacher (Sirotnik, 1988; Tikunoff and Ward, 1983). It is imperative that educational researchers understand the nature of classrooms and the concerns of teachers, and that they take these concerns into account when they identify research problems (and design programs of classroom research). Several changes in the roles of researchers and teachers can help to ensure that this goal is met. At a minimum, it is imperative that prospective classroom researchers spend time in classrooms, observing, talking with teachers and students, and attempting to understand classroom life from their perspectives. It may also be useful for them to experience what it is like to be a teacher, for example, by teaching in a public school classroom on an on-going basis for some portion of the school day (Hitchcock and Hughes, 1989; Lampert, 1985, 1990). Such direct participation in the world of teachers is likely to produce an appreciation of the problems they see as important and the conditions under which they may find proposed solutions to be useful.

A second strategy is to modify the teacher's role to include active involvement in the process of identifying research problems. One variation of teacher-researcher collaboration identified earlier in the chapter proposed that teachers or the public actually name the problems in need of study. Our preference is for a model of dialogue and negotiation, more in line with that proposed by Florio-Ruane (1989). We realize that such collaboration will not be easy. Our ideas for making it work are discussed in the final section of this chapter, which focuses on the importance of long-term commitments to school-based research and improvement programs.

Conducting Descriptive Research in Classrooms

Broadly speaking, descriptive classroom research has as its purpose the description and interpretation of specific aspects of classroom life, which are typically identified early in the research project. The implication is that a clear understanding of "what's going on" in a classroom will (among other things) contribute to understanding what kind of change is desirable and how change will be received. Because the focus of the research is on naturally occurring classrooms situations, with no attempt to change or modify existing practices, it is theoretically possible to conduct such research with no input or involvement on the part of teachers. Indeed, many early descriptive studies, which relied on observation forms developed a priori and used in a consistent way across classrooms, essentially did not involve teachers in the research enterprise [see, for example, Emmer, Evertson and Anderson (1980), Good and Grouws (1977)]. It is our position that, to increase the probability that such descriptive research will be useful and valuable to practitioners, teachers should have a role in the research process. This role might, but need not, include participation in data collection and analysis activities. However, at a minimum, it should include some input into decisions about the nature of the data to be collected and the range of occasions for data collection.

The Learning to Teach Mathematics project is illustrative of relatively minimal involvement by teachers in data-collection decisions. The project has as its purpose the description of novice teachers' knowledge, beliefs, thoughts, and actions in the classroom and influences on those characteristics. General guidelines for the collection of observational data were consistent across participants and sites, in that we observed each novice teaching mathematics for approximately one week at three periods of time during her final year of teacher preparation and first year of teaching. However, as we mentioned earlier in this chapter, researchers talked with the teachers prior to each observation. Information that the teachers provided about lesson objectives, planned activities, and specific concerns helped to focus the observations and to determine questions about the lesson that were asked during the postobservation interviews.

Staley's investigation of how basic skills were delivered in a classroom which featured process-centered instruction is another example of collaborative descriptive research (Staley, 1980; in Tikunoff and Ward, 1983). A central objective of the study was to identify when, where, and how basic skills instruction occurred in a classroom where such instruction was integrated into other curricular activities. Data (ethnographic field notes and videotapes of classroom interactions) were collected by the researchers. The teachers participated in data analysis. For example, collaborative analysis of the videotapes by the teachers, a principal, and the two university researchers verified the categories of classroom activities that contributed to learning basic skills which had been identified earlier by the researchers. Staley identified a number of outcomes of the research that he believed could not have occurred without the teachers' participation.

Conducting Intervention Research in Classrooms

Intervention research, in contrast to descriptive research, incorporates deliberate, systematic attempts on the part of the research team to change existing practice. It is our position that, for such research to be useful and valuable, the teachers who are involved must be active, willing, and informed participants. They must participate in the research by choice, and in ways that they perceive as maintaining their responsibilities and rights as teachers. Researchers must be respectful of teachers' professionalism and must treat them as partners rather than "subjects" in the research endeavor. Within these general guidelines, the nature and extent of teachers' participation in the design, implementation, and analysis of the intervention can vary greatly.

The CGI project and Heath's literacy project, described in previous chapters of the book, provide two different models of such researcher-teacher relationships. For example, the workshop for teachers in Phase 2 of the CGI project was explicitly designed based on the assumption that teachers are thoughtful professionals who construct their own knowledge and understanding. Teachers were not told to alter their teaching or their curriculum in specific ways. Rather, they were provided with access to knowledge about mathematics and about children's learning of mathematics and with support (e.g., materials, researchers' expertise) to modify their instructional programs to reflect that knowledge (Carpenter, Fennema, Peterson, Chiang, and Loef, 1989; Peterson, Carpenter, and Fennema, 1989).

As described in Chapter 4, Heath worked closely with teachers, both before she began her study and after she had interpreted its results. With the input of teachers, she designed the study, collected, and analyzed the data. Later, she made the data accessible to the teachers and worked with them to make curricular and other changes consistent with the findings of her research.

Paul Cobb and his colleagues struggled with the issue of how to develop a collaborative relationship with a teacher in their second-grade classroom teaching project. The initial phase of that project consisted of a "classroom teaching experiment" in which the researchers worked with one teacher to implement cognitively-based instructional activities in her classroom (Cobb, Yackel and Wood, 1988; Cobb, Wood and Yackel, 1990). Because the teacher was to be a teacher/researcher in the project, the university researchers felt it was important for her to understand the cognitive models of children's mathematical learning on which the instructional activities were based. They began meeting with her weekly in the spring prior to the experiment, to "discuss" the cognitive models and analyze video recordings of clinical interviews that had been conducted with her students at the beginning of the school year. However, Cobb realized that his conceptual analysis of the children's mathematical activity made little sense to the teacher. She viewed him as a "math professor" who knew a lot more than she did and as an evaluator of her answers. On the other hand, the researchers viewed the project teacher as attempting to learn by rote a list of technical terms, rather than to understand ideas of potential relevance to her classroom practice. All members of the research team had inadvertently contributed to the mutual construction of a social relationship inappropriate to the goals of the research project—a relationship that did not include the kinds of collaborative efforts that Cobb and colleagues envisioned as essential to the project's success. Cobb attempted to renegotiate the social norms of that relationship by initiating a dialogue about a topic within the domain of the teacher's expertise—her mathematics textbook. Through the dialogue, and resulting clinical interviews that the teacher conducted with her students, she began to see that the students had not learned the concepts she assumed they knew as a consequence of her textbook-based instruction. As Cobb and colleagues noted, "In retrospect, we see that our genuine collaboration with the project teacher began when she realized that her current instructional practices were problematic. She now viewed us as people [whom] she could work with to develop an alternative instructional approach. We had common problems and interests, and could engage in joint pedagogical problem solving" (Cobb et al., 1988, p. 131). The collaboration achieved by the research team enabled the teacher to modify her mathematics instruction in ways that made sense to her and were more in line with cognitive models of children's mathematical learning. This example illustrates the key role of factors such as shared commitments, common language, and on-going communication in successful teacher-researcher collaboration. It also points out the potential for collaboration to help assure that the standard of usefulness and value is met. [See also Florio-Ruane (1990), for a similar example of a negotiated relationship between teachers and researchers in a project to enhance the teaching of written literacy. Additional examples of teacher-researcher collaboration can be found in Sirotnik and Goodlad (1988).]

A LONG-TERM COMMITMENT TO SCHOOL IMPROVEMENT

In this final section of the chapter, we propose an approach to teacher-researcher collaboration that incorporates many of the ideas discussed above. In some ways, our ideas will be reminiscent of our earlier thinking about interdisciplinary collaboration. In other ways, they presage what we will say in the next chapter about standards for educational research practice.

First, from our own experience trying to collaborate, we think it likely that collaboration goes smoothly and easily only when everyone agrees to, or already shares, the same conventions [see also Becker (1991)]. However, it is highly unlikely that teachers and researchers will come to a collaborative research venture with the same conventions, expectations, or agenda.

In broad strokes then, teachers and researchers, trying to collaborate for the first time, will probably have an experience similar to ours: They will approach the arrangement with different commitments and speaking a different language; it will be difficult to communicate. Further, because the teacher and researcher come from different "occupational sectors," one of which does not usually engage in research, and another for which research is one of its primary activities [see Schensul and Schensul (1992)], they are likely to have many more differences to overcome than the two of us did.

Our ideas for promoting teacher-researcher collaboration center on increasing the possibilities for *joint* project work, some changes in the reward systems for both teachers and researchers, and making school issues a focal point for community argument and debate involving all stakeholders. First and foremost we want to encourage teachers and researchers to commit to improving schools for the long term. We do not expect that fruitful collaboration will occur easily or after a single study. About this, Huberman has written:

> . . . *the effects of a single study, however great, are limited and ephemeral ones; they decay. In fact, they decay more quickly unless both parties can stay together long enough to bridge from the findings to new or other areas . . . , to increased and more varied collaboration between researcher . . . and practitioner. . . . (Huberman, 1990, pp. 386–387)*

Second, both teachers and researchers must agree to listen to and debate each other's definition of the major practical problems to be solved within a particular school. In this process, we expect teachers to be most concerned and most articulate about immediate classroom practices, such as grouping, curriculum materials, and discipline. We expect researchers to be most concerned and most articulate about theories of learning, curriculum, social organization and structure, educational change, and the results of previous research. In other words each group will bring to the discussion expertise and concerns in the areas their occupations encourage them to learn and know best. From this starting point, the really hard work begins. If teachers and researchers are truly to benefit from each other's expertise, they must figure out ways to talk about what they know, to translate it back and forth, so that teachers' practical problems can be phrased in theoretical (disciplinary) terms, and researchers' theories can be exemplified in things that really happen in classrooms. All participants must enter into the discourse, stating their own beliefs, values, and interests; challenging each other's ideas and the bases on which they are held; and participating equally in controlling the discussion [see Sirotnik (1988)].

From this conjoining of expertise and interests, a "school research and improvement agenda" can emerge. We envision this agenda as a temporary and "contested" product. Although it will serve as an outline of important things to discover about the school, the agenda must be subject to modification as conditions change. As Sirotnik noted, "The trick, then, is to be explicit regarding the philosophy of any organizational or interorganizational effort . . . while at the same time being open to modification and revision of initial assumptions" (Sirotnik, 1988, p. 177). The agenda must also necessarily be one of compromises, because we have no reason to expect everyone concerned to agree on every agenda item. As indicated earlier, agreement or consensus seems an unlikely and largely unworkable standard if any agenda is to be timely and relevant to different constituencies and different interests. Rather, a commitment to a "working consensus," a majority decision in which dissenting views are duly acknowledged, is a more realistic goal (Oakes et al., 1986). The strength of a school research agenda seems to us to lie in its ability to represent diverse interests altogether in one document, thereby providing a more comprehensive picture of the issues, a guide for school-wide debate and decision-making as well as for coordinating research efforts, and an index of accumulated information for use by and within the school.

With few exceptions (and certainly with input from teachers and others), we think that researchers should be in charge of and responsible for the actual conduct of the research. Researchers have the time and are rewarded for doing research. They should already know the technical skills and the research norms to use in order to design credible research studies (see more on this in Chapter 7). Teachers may wish to learn about research, or may already be familiar with it; however, the daily teaching demands on their time and energy would seem to preclude their active and on-going involvement in activities such as data collection and analysis. The research projects by Heath, Cobb and colleagues, and Carpenter, Fennema, and Peterson are models for the kinds of teacher involvement we endorse.

As in these three research projects, we think that the success of a collaborative program of research and improvement depends on researchers who will commit to individual schools or groups of teachers for a long period of time. We cannot envision how research that will be relevant to schools can be conducted by a researcher here or there, a project that lasts a couple weeks or even a year. The circumstances and problems of classroom life are complex and have deep ties to the history and social conditions of our society. They will not be understood overnight. Nor will solutions or their acceptance be achieved overnight. If researchers are to conduct the work necessary to assist schools, they will have to stay in a school long enough to learn about and help to define the issues, to obtain good data, to analyze it, to interpret it to others, and to participate in discussions, debates, and decision-making about how best to address school problems in light of the data. It seems unavoidable for researchers who wish to do this to make a long-term commitment to particular schools.

If researchers are to make long-term commitments to schools, they will have to change the circumstances of their own work somewhat. For example, they will undoubtedly find themselves involved in a broader range of tasks than those associated with conducting other kinds of research. These tasks might include meetings with school personnel, inservice workshops, and other formal and informal contacts with school and community stakeholders. Thus, the time and energy necessary for productive collaboration is likely to take away from researchers' time to analyze data and to write articles for publication. And, it will not be easy to pick up and move to another academic job in a faraway location.

Teachers' work situations will also be changed. Their involvement in research activities will similarly require additional meetings and workshops. And, their planning and preparation, as well as actual classroom teaching, will be influenced by the presence of researchers and the nature of the investigation. Like researchers, they will undoubtedly find that productive collaboration takes away from time available for other aspects of their professional lives.

Another implication of our position is that some school and classroom problems are not good candidates for educational research. If teachers and researchers are to devote long hours and many years to the improvement of education through research, it seems desirable for them to tackle the "big issues," and as Scriven has suggested, the issues about which something can conceivably be done (Scriven, 1986). If the problems studied are likely to produce results that are very expensive, politically infeasible, or for which there are no practical alternatives, then they would appear—at least on the surface—to be poor candidates. At the least, participants should be aware of such limitations when selecting classroom problems to investigate.

In sum, we endorse opportunities for teachers and researchers to work together on studies of relevance and importance to both. We think that such collaborations can increase the likelihood that the results of classroom research will find their way into classroom practice. We expect that the collaborations will be productive if members of each group understand and take into account their differences, work hard to overcome them, and learn to appreciate and rely on the respective strengths of each group. We also expect that both teachers and researchers will have to devote considerable time and energy to make the collaboration a success.

Finally, we want to encourage teachers and researchers to debate, negotiate, and decide what problems to study, how to conduct the study, and how to use the results of studies. One of the most consistent themes in the literature on teacher-researcher collaboration is the importance of communication—debate and negotiation—throughout the research process. As

Sirotnik stated, "Clearly, at the heart of collaborative inquiry is the willingness and ability of people to engage in competent discourse and communication" (Sirotnik, 1988, p. 176). We think the occasions for teachers and researchers to participate in such competent discourse can be further enhanced if certain standards for educational research are known and agreed upon by both groups. We turn, in the next chapter, to a proposed set of such standards.

► 7

Standards of Validity for Classroom Research[1]

A GENERAL CONCEPTION OF VALIDITY IN EDUCATIONAL RESEARCH

Lee Shulman has written,

> ... education is a field of study, *a locus containing phenomena, events, institutions, problems, persons, and processes, which themselves constitute the raw material for inquiries of many kinds. The perspectives and procedures of many disciplines can be brought to bear on the questions arising from and inherent in education as a field of study. As each of these disciplinary perspectives is brought to bear on the field of education, it brings with it its own set of concepts, methods, and procedures, often modifying them to fit the phenomena or problems of education.* (Shulman, 1988a, p. 5, Shulman's emphasis).

Because educational research draws on many different disciplines for theoretical or conceptual frameworks, employs various frameworks depending on research purposes, uses an assortment of "research designs" (organized and standardized sets of procedures for gathering and analyzing data such as experimental design, survey design, or ethnographic design), and adopts different conventions for reporting results, standards for evaluating educational research are extremely important. Some set of standards seems necessary, otherwise we have no clear means of comparing various studies; no good procedure for deciding which results we can trust; no credible way to take action based on research results.

However, when we attempt to define a set of standards, a problem arises almost immediately. If different frameworks lead to different research questions and different research designs, and if each specific framework/research questions/design combination has its own internal logic and specific set of standards for conduct, then what general standards can be used and how can they be used? Defining general standards that are simultaneously relevant to a wide range of studies, meaningful (not so vague and abstract as to be met by any study that calls itself one), and respectful of the fact that frameworks, research questions, and research designs are constantly undergoing revision and change, is extremely difficult to do.

In an article in *Educational Researcher*, Howe and Eisenhart proposed a set of general standards for educational research (Howe and Eisenhart, 1990). They envisioned these standards as preliminary ones that would raise the issue of general standards for educational research and generate discussion of it. They also envisioned the standards as *rules of thumb*, not requirements cast in stone, that might guide the conduct, assessment, and reporting of educational research.

More recently, Eisenhart and Howe applied their general standards to the issue of validity of educational research studies (Eisenhart and Howe, 1992). Validity—generally conceived as the trustworthiness of a research study—has usually been defined in terms of the logic and technical adequacy of the process used to conduct a study; that is, conventional validity refers specifically to a level of confidence in the accuracy and appropriateness of the methods used in an investigation [see, for example, Campbell and Stanley (1963), Smith and Glass (1987)].

This definition of validity was worked out with specific reference to experimental research designs. Within the context of experimental research, validity was seen as having two components: internal and external. Internal validity refers to the legitimacy of the inference that an experimental treatment causes certain effects. External validity refers to the legitimacy of generalizing the effects observed in one situation to other populations and settings (Eisenhart and Howe, 1992, pp. 644–645).

Eisenhart and Howe pointed out that the emergence of nonexperimental, so-called "qualitative," methods in educational research posed new questions about validity and how it should be defined. In particular, questions were raised about the appropriateness of applying the conventional conception of validity to nonexperimental research designs and about what alternative standards might reasonably be applied to these alternative designs.

The approach to validity suggested by Eisenhart and Howe is more inclusive than the conventional definition. They argued that the validity of an educational research study, regardless of the research design used, can be determined by how carefully the study is designed, conducted, and presented; how sensitively it treats human subjects; and how well it contributes to important educational issues, including debates about educational theory and practice.

Eisenhart and Howe made two additional proposals that are especially relevant to this chapter. First, in an attempt to avoid the tendency to privilege certain kinds of research studies (for example, experimental over non-experimental designs, or "quantitative" over "qualitative" studies), they proposed that *all* research studies be conceived of as *arguments* [following Dunn (1982); House (1977)]—where *argument* is defined as a discussion involving different points of view. The metaphor of research study-as-argument is useful in educational research for two major reasons (Dunn, 1982).

First, the metaphor creates a level playing field on which various research designs and their results may be considered of equal importance, at least as a point of departure. If all research studies are thought of as arguments for a particular set of findings, then all studies may be considered provisionally equivalent, regardless of disciplinary perspective or methodology. As Dunn put it, the metaphor of research study *qua* argument discourages the "patently false conclusion that knowledge derived from one source is inherently superior" (Dunn, 1982, p. 295).

Second, the metaphor encourages the idea that the results of research should be matters of public debate and scrutiny. When research studies are viewed as arguments, it is straightforward to expect that the results of research studies will be made accessible to the public, and that they will be assessed, compared, corrected, and perhaps reinterpreted to guide decision-making or policy.

Eisenhart and Howe also proposed that a valid argument be defined as one that is legitimate in two interrelated ways: a general way and a design-specific way. Characterizing all educational research studies in terms of the general concept of an argument leads rather straightforwardly to a general concept of validity that can be applied across all such arguments regardless of their particular contents [see Messick (1989) for the application of this conception of validity to testing practice]. On the other hand, judgments regarding the validity of a particular argument also depend on whether the argument is acceptable to scholars trained in and working within a specific tradition of research (disciplinary, theoretical, or methodological); judgments of research validity must allow the kinds of evidence and associated principles employed in particular arguments to vary substantially. Thus, the overall validity of an educational research study is operationally determined by a global assessment of how well it measures up both to ecumenical, general standards and to design-specific standards.

In this chapter, we review Eisenhart and Howe's standards and use them to assess the work that we (Eisenhart and Borko) have done together. We also use them to assess the work of several other educational researchers including the exemplars of research in cognitive psychology and educational anthropology that we featured in Chapters 3 and 4. We believe that these standards can serve as useful rules of thumb for thinking about, designing, and evaluating the many different kinds of research studies being done in classrooms. Without these standards or some others like them to guide our assessment of research studies, we are afraid that we have only a disparate group of classroom studies (using different frameworks, research questions, and research designs) about the same topic, e.g., teaching and learning reading, or teaching and learning mathematics, with no clear way to compare or debate their relative merits and interconnections. At the end of the chapter, we make a third, related proposal, also inspired by the work of Dunn: When various research studies are conceived of as arguments and comparable standards are systematically applied to them, their relative merits and contributions to educational policy, practice, and reform can be more fully considered, debated, and decided in the public arena than has heretofore been the case or norm.

In this chapter, we focus on Eisenhart and Howe's general standards only. In earlier chapters, when we presented our own work and several other exemplars, we indicated how each study measured up to design-specific criteria within its own tradition. Here we find that our own study, as well as the studies we described as exemplars of design-specific approaches in cognitive psychology and educational anthropology, fall somewhat short when appraised by Eisenhart and Howe's standards.

The limitations of our exemplars are particularly obvious with regard to Eisenhart and Howe's Standards 1, 4 and 5. Standard 1 requires researchers to provide more information than is conventionally included in a research report about the literature background and the researcher commitments that informed the development and design of the study. Standards 4 and 5 require researchers to include discussions of worth and value—discussions that also are commonly omitted from research reports. These elements of the three standards are necessary to make the research more accessible and potentially useful to a wider audience than has previously been the target for educational research results. Thus, in each case where our exemplars fall short, it is because we are adding requirements that we think are important, but that conventionally have not been used to evaluate educational research. None of the studies we described—our own work or the exemplars—was originally conceived with these general standards in mind.[2]

Before turning to the standards themselves, one additional caveat is in order. It is important to keep in mind that Eisenhart and Howe did not intend these standards to be a list of discrete items that readers of research would apply independently, one at a time. Rather, each standard should be seen as a part of an overlapping set, to be considered simultaneously, as one evaluates the validity of a research project. When the standards are applied as a set, it becomes apparent that compromises are inevitable. In a given study the importance of meeting one standard may outweigh the value of another. Similarly, characteristics that result in high marks when a study is judged according to one standard may become costs or risks in light of other standards.

Eisenhart and Howe's first three standards are rules of thumb for systematic consideration of research studies *qua* arguments.[3] Thus, they may be appropriately invoked across substantially different arguments, even though their precise application in a given study requires sophisticated and specialized knowledge particular to that study. The fourth and fifth standards address more global requirements, whose application is not necessarily dictated in ways that are peculiar to specific (at least conventional) research designs.

Standard 1: Contribution to Knowledge in the Field

For research studies to satisfy this standard, they must be part of, and build upon, some tradition of scholarship—be it scholarship in the area of educational theory, practice, or both. Another way to say this is the study's (potential) contribution to debates about educational theory or practice must be clear. Further, in order that a study's contribution can be fairly judged, the assumptions and goals embedded in the development and conduct of that study must be made explicit and justified.

Jacob recently made a similar point (Jacob, 1990). She noted that discussions of research designs in educational research often ignore the assumptions behind the designs. "Designs and methods often are presented as if they objectively determined truth and were independent of frameworks that generated them. This serves only to mask the underlying assumptions that frame the research" (Jacob, 1990, p. 196). We would add that only when the assumptions behind the selection of research questions and methods are unmasked can the arguments derived from a study be placed in their appropriate context and the arguments of one study appropriately compared to those of other studies.

As discussed in Chapter 6, existing knowledge in education has at least two major variants: what researchers know and believe from their work and experiences; and what practitioners know and believe from their work and experiences.[4] At any given point in time, for any given topic, these two variants of "background knowledge" may be quite far apart. Smith and Shepard, for example, in their studies of kindergarten retention practices found that although empirical research consistently shows a weak or negative relationship between academic performance and grade retention, many teachers, administrators, and parents believe wholeheartedly in the practice (Smith and Shepard, 1987).

Whether some social science theory is used to generate research questions and design, or whether a study is designed to address teacher-identified issues, background knowledge—theoretical or empirical knowledge derived from previous research and/or the craft knowledge of teachers and other interested parties—should be made explicit and accessible as a guide for readers to understand the development of research questions and the choice of methods. Further, a research study must be placed within the context of both sets of assumptions (theoretical/empirical and craft), to assure that it will be seen as contributing to knowledge by both communities —the community of researchers, and the community of teachers.

Perhaps less obvious but nonetheless a crucial part of background knowledge is the researcher's own prior knowledge, or "subjectivity" (Peshkin, 1988). Peshkin has argued that subjectivity is the basis for the researcher's distinctive contribution, which comes from joining personal interpretations with the data that have been collected and analyzed. As with assumptions derived from the literature, subjectivities must be made explicit if they are to advance, rather than obscure, the validity of research *qua* argument.

In sum, for research studies to be valid in terms of Standard 1, background assumptions must be made explicit so that the study's connections to previous knowledge and its potential contribution to knowledge will be clear. We have previously discussed our theoretical commitments and prior experiences as they related to our work on the Learning to Teach Mathematics project. We would venture to say that we have spent more pages in print on these topics than any other researchers we know. However, we have not placed our work within the context of craft knowledge of teaching or of learning to teach.

The CGI project meets one component of this standard in an exemplary fashion. That is, the project is strongly grounded in theoretical and empirical scholarship on student and teacher cognition. The theoretical frameworks that guided development of the inservice workshop and data-collection instruments were explicitly identified by the researchers (see Chapter 3). However, other components of the standard are not so strongly met. The researchers did not explicitly connect their work to the craft knowledge of teachers (although the inservice workshop certainly was designed to be sensitive to that knowledge base by providing suggestions for the teachers to adapt rather than prescriptions for them to adopt). Nor did they reveal their own subjectivities or prior experiences, other than to acknowledge the roles that Carpenter played in the development of the taxonomy of addition and subtraction problem types and Peterson played in the conceptualization of teachers as thoughtful professionals. These omissions are not surprising, given common practice in cognitive psychological research.

Ways with Words also does not meet this standard as strongly as it might. Although Heath establishes her research problem by reference to previous work in sociolinguistics, one has to infer that Heath also was guided by cultural difference theory as she planned, conducted, and later described her work. She did not make explicit the conceptual connections between her study and other scholarship about cultural differences. Nor did she present in any detail her own prior commitments or subjectivities. We think she could have done these things, but we also know that existing conventions of ethnographic methodology and reporting did not necessarily call for such connections or disclosures (note that they are nowhere part of Spindler's criteria for a good ethnography). In this light, it is interesting to recall that at the end of her book, Heath seemed to recognize that her findings were not fully interpretable in terms of cultural difference theory, yet she did not offer an alternate, more powerful theory. We think Heath's failure to discuss this theoretical quandary diminishes somewhat the (albeit considerable) contribution of her book. Also, because the positive impact of Heath's findings on the teachers in her study had eroded by the time she wrote the end of the book, many practitioners, who are inspired as they read the earlier chapters, become disheartened by its end. We find this outcome unfortunate, too, and think that Heath might have enhanced her book's contribution to educational practice if she had suggested some (potential) ways to prevent the erosion.

Standard 2: The Fit Between Research Questions, Data-Collection Procedures, and Analysis Techniques

Standard 2 states that the data-collection techniques and the data-analysis procedures ought to fit, or be suitable for answering, the research questions asked. Another way to say this is research questions ought to drive data-collection techniques and analysis rather than vice versa.

This standard emphasizes the importance of deciding what research questions the study will address *before* deciding what research design is appropriate or best to use. Research questions inevitably demand certain kinds of data and analyses of them, and scholars consider some research designs much better choices than others for obtaining specific kinds of data and conducting appropriate analyses. Further, research designs sometimes must be modified, combined, even created in order to address the research questions being studied.[5]

Correctly ordering research questions and methods, and developing their fit, is, of course, a complex issue. We do not mean to suggest that researchers can proceed as if they are blank slates—free of prior methodological interests, commitments, or expertise. Neither can they behave as if they have super intellects—capable of competently choosing from all of the relevant questions and methodologies. Nor, finally, can they operate as if they had available infinite time, resources, or expertise. In some sense, then, research design will indeed affect research questions. On the other hand, the degree to which this occurs should be minimized. Research studies *qua* arguments have questionable validity when methodological preferences or matters of convenience, rather than research questions, drive the study. Valid studies require designs that have been cogently developed from research questions.

In our work together on the Learning to Teach Mathematics project, we think this standard was quite explicitly considered and met. Perhaps because our different disciplinary traditions prompted us to generate distinctly different research questions and our original confusion about whether or how to compromise led us back to our disciplines for guidance (see Chapters 3 and 4), the set of research questions we eventually used had to be carefully articulated and then debated by members of our research team. Our research design had to be crafted so that all team members could understand how the design would permit us to address each question. Our data-collection instruments and procedures were varied, and they were developed or selected on the basis of the research questions and design. Looking back now, we think we gave explicit attention to these matters primarily because we were part of an interdisciplinary team that was trying to communicate and collaborate (see Chapter 5), not because we had any incipient concerns about the validity of our work at the time.

In the case of the CGI project, the major research questions in Phase 1 focused on the relationships among teachers' pedagogical content knowledge, their pedagogical content beliefs, and student achievement. The purpose of Phase 2 was to study the effects of an inservice program designed to provide teachers with detailed knowledge about children's knowledge and thinking on teachers' knowledge, beliefs, and instructional practices and on students' achievement, confidence, and beliefs. Data-collection techniques included a variety of questionnaires, interviews, observation systems, and student achievement measures. Most of these instruments were constructed specifically for the project, and they were clearly suitable for answering the research questions. For example, measures of teachers' pedagogical content beliefs were based on a framework of four assumptions about children's learning of mathematics derived from the researchers' review of scholarly literature (Peterson, Fennema, Carpenter, and Loef, 1989; see also Chapter 3). Student achievement was assessed using a set of instruments that included a widely used standardized achievement test as well as several scales and interview protocols constructed specifically for the study, based on the taxonomy of problem types and children's solution processes that served as the basis for the inservice intervention (see Chapter 3). This approach of using both standardized and project-specific measures addresses commonly voiced concerns about using standardized achievement tests as measures of teacher effectiveness (Shavelson et al., 1986). Although the researchers did not explicitly state that research questions were identified before the research design and instruments were developed, the close match among these components of the project and the fact that the instruments were developed specifically for the project lead us to conclude that Standard 2 was met in an exemplary fashion.

The research questions for Heath's study in *Ways with Words* were inspired by questions that her university education students raised in class: "What were the effects of preschool home and community environments on the learning of those language structures and uses which were needed in classrooms and job settings?" (Heath, 1983, p. 2) and, given the obvious differences in language use and behavior of students from different communities or cultural groups, why didn't researchers "describe children learning to use language as they grew up in their own community culture?" (Heath, 1983, p. 3). Adopting an ethnographic research design, Heath pursued these questions in her study. Considering Heath's need to study communities, their daily language use, and how they raised their children over time, it is hard to imagine a more appropriate design for her research questions.

Standard 3: The Effective Application of Specific Data-Collection and Analysis Techniques

In addition to deriving coherently from research questions, data-collection and analysis techniques must be competently applied, in a more-or-less technical sense. Research studies *qua* arguments cannot be valid without credible reasons for a specific choice of subjects and competent application of data-gathering procedures and analysis techniques. Various principles guide how interviews should be conducted, how instruments should be designed, how sampling should proceed, how data should be reduced, and so forth, such that findings are rendered credible. If credibility is not achieved at this level, then the more general (and more important) conclusions that ultimately rest on the findings will be suspect.

It is not the case that educational researchers must create brand new principles and procedures for competently conducting their work. Principles and systematic procedures for the conduct and assessment of numerous qualitative and quantitative research designs have been formulated and debated for years within the social science disciplines. Although some modification of technical standards from the social sciences may be necessary for educational research purposes, it is incumbent on educational researchers—if they wish to demonstrate that their techniques have been competently applied—to locate their work in the historical, disciplinary, or traditional contexts in which their methods were developed.

In Learning to Teach Mathematics (LTTM), we employed techniques that have been widely used for classroom research in the traditions of cognitive psychology (stimulated recall interviews, planning-observation-reflection data-collection cycles, etc.) and educational anthropology (classroom observations, open-ended interviewing, etc.). However, it is important to point out that our use of these techniques in LTTM does not follow strictly the canons of conventional methodology in either of the two disciplines.

In cognitive psychology, for example, the stimulated recall method typically consists of replaying a videotape or audiotape of the target event (e.g., a classroom lesson) to enable the participant to recall and report on his or her thoughts during that event. Protocols from stimulated recall sessions are then analyzed using content analysis methods. The videotape or audiotape provides explicit, informationally rich cues to stimulate the participant's recall of the event. The likelihood of producing valid data (e.g., with maximal completeness and minimal distortion) is increased when probes are not used or are very general in nature (Shavelson et al., 1986; see Chapter 3). We were unable to use stimulated recall in an optimal fashion for several reasons. First, time constraints prevented us from replaying the audiotaped lessons for participants during the postlesson interviews. Instead, we provided verbal descriptions of specific events within the lessons, based on our hand-written observation notes. Second, to ensure comparable data across participants and situations, we asked a series of explicit, predetermined questions about participants' thinking during the targeted events. Thus, our probes did request that the teachers search their long-term memory for specific information. These constraints increased the potential for data distortion and made the study less than ideal as a cognitive psychological investigation of teachers' thinking during instruction.

In educational anthropology, classic ethnographic methodology would require us to meet the criteria set forth by Spindler (Spindler, 1982; see Chapter 4 this book). We were unable to do this fully for several reasons. First, limited time and money prevented us from being in the schools and university with the student teachers on a full-time basis. Second, several different researchers were responsible for collecting comparable data from different study participants and at different locations. These constraints also led us to select or develop all but a few of our constructs and instruments beforehand. In addition, the time we could spend with the student teachers had to be apportioned to collecting specific information about pedagogy, cognition, and mathematics, as well as about the sociocultural knowledge that the student teachers had and created.

The constraints under which we operated dilute the strength of our study as classic ethnographic research and render the sociocultural information we did collect more superficial than desirable in ethnographic research. They also caused the information about teachers' thinking to be less extensive and potentially more distorted than is desirable in cognitive psychological research. However, we think that these limitations were offset by the study's enhanced power to address a wider range of current issues in mathematics education than would be possible from the standpoint of classic ethnography or cognitive psychology alone.

Characteristics of the CGI study reported in the numerous journal articles and book chapters written about the project suggest that it meets standards for good, experimental cognitive psychological research. All 40 participating teachers were volunteers, a situation that is not ideal with respect to the canons of experimental research design, but is typically unavoidable and certainly acceptable practice in classroom research. However, the teachers were randomly assigned (by school, also acceptable practice) to treatment and control conditions. To ensure the reliability—i.e., the consistency or dependability of measurement across settings—of observational data, observation manuals were developed for each observation system. Classroom observers were trained in a two-week training session and were tested for both content knowledge and coding ability; only those observers who achieved the criterion levels on both tests were judged sufficiently knowledgeable and skilled to conduct classroom observations. In addition, interobserver agreement was checked at scheduled times during data collection. Similar care was taken in other aspects of the research design and implementation. Although some readers might wish for more information about data-collection instruments and analysis procedures, such information is rarely provided in journal articles due to strict page considerations.

In Heath's study, she used classic ethnography as her research design. Her study appears to meet all the standards for good ethnographic research outlined by Spindler. Heath also went beyond Spindler's criteria when she helped the teachers use her findings, observed their efforts, and then used these results to extend her conclusions. Apparently she intervened in what might be called "classic ethnographic fashion;" that is, she intervened only *after* she had collected and analyzed the bulk of her data, established her findings, and drawn tentative conclusions. [See the work of Roman (1989) and Roman and Apple (1990) for an illustration of a more radical form of current ethnography wherein the researcher is actively involved in helping to change participants from the beginning of the study.]

Standard 4: Value Constraints

Valid research studies *qua* arguments must include discussion of values, i.e., the importance or usefulness of the study and its risks. The conduct of educational research is subject to both "external" and "internal" value constraints.

External Value Constraints   External value constraints have to do with whether the research is valuable for informing and improving educational practice—the "so what?" question. Research might be well designed and conducted in a *technical* sense but that alone is an insufficient criterion of value. Valid studies must also be worthwhile. With this standard, we explicitly include the issue raised in Chapter 6—use and importance of research findings to practitioners—as a criterion for good educational research.

The concern with worthwhile issues, when considered in the context of educational practice, has several implications. One is that research investigations be comprehensive enough to address and expose the important and profound problems and issues that arise for practitioners. This is not primarily a matter of increasing the scope of research projects so that more data can be collected and analyzed, or of developing sophisticated technical means for more rapidly and precisely handling data. Rather, it means committing the educational research community to multifaceted investigations of major educational issues—whether they be at the level of pedagogy, policy, or social theory—and then demanding that researchers ground their methodology in the nature of these issues.

Admittedly, judgments of the worth of research projects can be very difficult to make. They have the potential to be exceedingly biased, as anyone who has served on a human subjects committee can attest. However, these are not judgments from which researchers can (or do) forever duck [witness the exchange in *Educational Researcher* between Finn and Shavelson and Berliner in which they debated whether educational research has or has not made an important contribution to the improvement of educational practice, Finn (1988); Shavelson and Berliner (1988); also see the more recent discussion in *Educational Researcher* by Jackson (1990a)]. Researchers are best advised to put questions about the worth of research immediately on the table, lest implicit judgments about worth or lack of it operate behind the scenes, as a kind of hidden agenda. Clearly, even if others might be puzzled about the study's worth, educational researchers themselves ought to be able to communicate what value their research has (if only potentially) for educational practice.

The conclusions of educational research also ought to be accessible to interested people who do not ordinarily read research journals or who find the language of research journals hard to decipher. That is, researchers should present their work in publications, conferences, or other forums read or attended by practitioners and policy-makers. In addition, the language of the results and implications should be cast in a form that is understandable to, and debatable by, various audiences (those who might read accounts of the research) or stakeholders (those who have a material interest in the results or uses of the research)—teachers, administrators, parents, and also educational researchers with varying perspectives and expertise. Accordingly, researchers must give attention to the social, political, and cultural features of the contexts and individuals they investigate and to which the results might be applied (Erickson, 1986; House, 1980, Chapter 12; Weiss, 1983). For example, if politically controversial results are to be seriously considered by stakeholders, then researchers must give attention to how they report such results to the public. Researchers must also be sensitive to the inevitably value-laden language that they employ— terms like "at risk," or "culturally different"—to avoid mystifying their findings and cloaking them in a false "scientific objectivity."

Valid research studies *qua* arguments, then, should explicitly address, in language that is generally accessible to the community of interested parties, the importance of the research and its (potential) usefulness. This requirement facilitates and encourages public debate of educational issues and of the implications of research results.

For us, this standard is especially crucial because it underscores that consideration of important questions is more consequential than choice of methodology. The important questions may not, for example, lend themselves to an elegant experimental procedure lifted step-by-step from a methods textbook. As we alluded to earlier in our assessment of the Learning to Teach Mathematics project under Standard 3, many questions that meet these criteria are not necessarily easily addressed using the classic or patented research designs that appear in textbooks. Consider also, for example, the questions that Eisenhart and her colleagues raised in a study of a desegregating elementary school: What is the meaning of race at this school (Clement et al., 1979)? What is the meaning of gender at this school (Eisenhart and Holland, 1983)? Consider also the question that we are attempting to answer in our study of mathematics teachers: How do student teachers learn to be teachers, and what influences their learning?

To answer such questions in a way that is comprehensive, that "speaks" to various relevant audiences, and that facilitates public debate probably means that classic or conventional research designs will need to be modified. Reasoned alternatives to classic designs may be necessary to address the particulars of a given research question at a given point in time. Conventional designs might have to be traded away for breadth of coverage that speaks to the concerns of different audiences, for example. This is a tradeoff we made in the Learning to Teach Mathematics project. It remains to be demonstrated whether our tradeoff can be translated into findings that are widely useful for public debate about mathematics education.

In our judgment, the CGI project addresses external value constraints very well. The goal of the curriculum development component of the project, to develop an inservice program designed to improve teachers' classroom instruction and children's achievement in mathematics, is certainly a worthwhile one, and one that speaks directly to the improvement of educational practice. The extensive written communication about the project has been addressed both to the educational research community (see references cited in Chapter 3) and to practicing teachers and administrators (Fennema and Carpenter, 1989; Loef et al., 1988; Peterson et al., 1988). In addition, members of the research team have provided, and have trained others to provide, inservice workshops for teachers based on the workshop that was developed and tested within the original CGI project. They also have spoken at numerous and varied national association meetings. Thus, it seems reasonable to conclude that research findings and conclusions have been made accessible to a wide audience of educational researchers, practitioners, and policy-makers.

We think that the study described in *Ways with Words* is clearly worthwhile. Few practitioners or educational researchers would deny the importance of learning more about the linguistic and sociocultural factors in community life that contribute to children's successes or failures in school. The book has been widely read, as evidenced by its numerous reprintings, and Heath is in great demand as a speaker and a consultant to programs for practicing teachers. Unfortunately, as already discussed, the book's contribution to various audiences and public debate seems to be diminished somewhat by the lack of a theoretical and practical finale.

Internal Value Constraints   Internal value constraints refer to research ethics. Howe and Eisenhart call research ethics "internal" because they have to do with the *way* research is conducted vis-a-vis research subjects, not with the (external) value or use of results.

As may be the case with external value constraints, attending to internal constraints sometimes requires tradeoffs against other aspects of validity. For instance, in the Learning to Teach Mathematics study, teachers had input into decisions about the dates and classes we would observe. In more conventional observation studies, teachers typically do not know when observations will occur, because researchers do not want teachers to alter their teaching for the observer. Because our participants were novice teachers and our observation work was intensive (one week of observations three times per year, plus pre- and postobservation interviews each day), we thought it was important to trade away the possibility of observing a "natural" classroom (at least on the first day) for the teachers' rights to negotiate observation times. Further, we hoped that the intensity and extensiveness of observations would minimize the probability that what we saw would be atypical. Concerns such as these are especially relevant to educational researchers because they must weigh the quality of the data they can gather (and whether they can gather any data at all) against principles such as individual rights, informed consent, privacy, and confidentiality.

In classroom research, one special internal value constraint arises because the researcher is not really an uninvolved stranger. Unlike the classic ethnographer or the classic experimenter, classroom researchers have direct knowledge of classrooms (having been students and, often, teachers themselves) and typically are recognized by participants as having some expertise with respect to the issues being investigated or potentially investigated. A tension arises when participants seek the advice or feedback of the researcher, when the research design places the researcher in the role of a non-participant observer. Such a tension was encountered in our work in the Learning to Teach Mathematics study. The four researchers who collected data during the classroom observation cycles all had previous experience as classroom teachers and supervisors of student teachers. When observing student teaching, we often did see ways in which the participants could improve their teaching. And, the participants often asked us questions about how to teach particularly tricky concepts, despite our initial characterization of our roles as researchers, not advisors. In some cases, we felt ethically compelled to provide advice. In others, we wanted to give feedback but did not feel so compelled. At any rate, the tension existed throughout the project, without any easy solution.

In the case of intervention research, the researchers also have a desired outcome in mind. Then, the tension is of a different kind. University people often consider themselves the experts in what can or should happen in classrooms. That is, they have a body of content that they want to communicate to teachers for implementation. On the other hand, many also believe in teacher empowerment; that is, that teachers should be permitted an equal voice with researchers, should participate as equals in conversations and debates about the direction of educational practice, and should be able to make up their own minds about how to think about and practice their craft. What kind of relationship should researchers have with research participants such as teachers? How should teachers and other research participants be treated in intervention studies?

Some of our ideas about roles and relationships of teachers and researchers in intervention studies were presented in Chapter 6. In that chapter, research programs by Heath, Cobb and colleagues, and Carpenter, Fennema and Peterson were discussed as models of collaborative relationships that attempt to take into account the expertise, interests, and concerns of both researchers and teachers. The reader may wish to refer back to our discussion of the study by Cobb and colleagues because it illustrates a research study in which the university researchers and classroom teacher explicitly confronted the problem of creating a "genuine collaboration" that respected both the goals of the researchers and the interests and concerns of the teacher.

V. Richardson and Anders faced a different issue in teacher-researcher relationships in their study of a staff development project on reading comprehension (Richardson and Anders, 1990). Throughout the project, Richardson and Anders experienced a tension between: 1) a desire for the staff development process to become "owned" by the teachers involved; and 2) a desire for the staff development content to focus on the researchers' best ideas (taken from the literature) about how to teach reading comprehension. The tension was exacerbated by the teachers' inclination, learned in their previous experiences with staff development, to permit and indeed want the researchers to lead the staff development (one teacher is quoted as saying, "Just tell us about a neat practice—something you think is a good idea"). The teachers also considered it the researchers' job to lead: "You people at the University have the time to go to the library and figure these things out; then you can just come and tell us what we should do" (Richardson and Anders, 1990, p. 12). And the researchers were ambivalent about their roles: Should they lead or not? When should they? When not? After considerable time and, in at least one case, a serious confrontation between the researchers and the teachers, some progress was made in diminishing the "expert" role of the researcher and expanding the purview of the "teacher" role. However, the fundamental tension remained; at least within the span of this study, the teachers and researchers did not seem to achieve the kind of shared purpose that Cobb and colleagues describe (see Chapter 6).

Both the Cobb et al. and the Richardson and Anders studies beg the ethical questions of what opportunities teachers really have to disagree with or reject research findings and what obligations researchers have to honor teachers' views on these matters. For example, what happens if, despite the most persuasive presentations of evidence by researchers of the dangers or noneffects of an educational practice—e.g., tracking, special education placements, early retentions (Shepard, 1991)—practitioners continue to believe in the practice or to think that it is worthwhile and continue to practice it? This type of teacher "resistance" (Florio-Ruane and Lensmire, 1990; Howe, 1992) is quite evident, as illustrated in beginning teachers' reluctance to give up their folk beliefs about classroom control (Florio-Ruane and Lensmire, 1990), many experienced teachers' disinclination to stop the practice of kindergarten retention (Smith and Shepard, 1987), and most teachers' preference for tracking (Oakes, 1985). In each case, the practice has been repeatedly and consistently shown by researchers to be detrimental or to have no effect, yet practitioners continue to believe in it and practice it.

At the present time, we do not see any resolution of this issue. Although the discrepancy between research evidence and practice is easy to spot, few have proposed an approach to resolving the conflict. Howe suggested that simply facing the issue, with a commitment to ethical behavior, is a lesser of evils between the positivist extreme that gives the scientific expert the authority (right to overrule) and the interpretivist extreme that gives the participants ultimate authority (Howe, 1992). In brief, he recommended that researchers and teachers learn to collaborate in ways that recognize the strengths (and limitations) of scientific and participant knowledge and together figure out how to build upon both kinds of existing knowledge to resolve a particular practice issue. We think that such issues of internal value require considerably more attention in educational research than has heretofore been the norm.

Returning to our two exemplary studies, we find that the CGI project addressed at least some of these internal value constraints. The format of the inservice workshop was based on the assumption that teachers are thoughtful professionals who construct their own knowledge and understanding. Participants were provided with access to information about student cognition but were given the choice as to whether and how they would incorporate that information into their classroom instruction. Although the term "teacher empowerment" was not used by the researchers, the assumption clearly was that teachers are able to, and should be trusted to, make up their own minds about how to think about and practice their craft. However, teachers did not have an equal voice with researchers in designing the inservice program. The content was set; their choices were about how to utilize that content. Also, to our knowledge, the researchers did not explicitly attend to building a relationship of mutual trust with the teachers who participated in the project. Perhaps trust-building activities were incorporated into the workshops for experimental and control teachers, but they were not described in publications reporting on the project.

In Heath's book, it is very hard to determine what internal value constraints were faced or handled. As in so many other reports of research, these issues were not dealt with explicitly in the book. We assume that Heath faced various problems associated with maintaining confidentiality, respecting privacy, and being sensitive to the positions of the people she studied; however, we do not hear about these matters in her text. As we have indicated above, we think it is necessary for researchers to begin to share information about these topics in print.

Standard 5: Comprehensiveness

Our fifth standard—comprehensiveness—encompasses responding in a holistic way to the first four standards, balancing them, and going beyond them. We mean "comprehensiveness" in three senses. First, with regard to Standards 1–3, Standard 5 demands a judgment about the overall contribution, clarity, coherence, and competence—what might also be called "overall theoretical and technical quality"—of the research process and the outcomes of a study. Second, with respect to Standards 1–4, Standard 5 requires a balancing of the overall technical quality, the value and importance of the study, and the risks involved in the study. As indicated above, meeting one standard, such as addressing a particularly important research question or assuring the protection of human subjects, may require trade-offs against other standards. This second aspect of Standard 5 calls for thoughtful consideration and explanation of such tradeoffs.

Third, Standard 5 requires comprehensiveness in the sense of being alert to and able to employ knowledge from outside the particular perspective and tradition within which one is working, and being able to apply general principles for evaluating arguments. Denzin, Goetz and LeCompte, and Shulman argued that "triangulation by theory"—or application of various explanations to the data at hand and selection of the most plausible one to "explain" the research results—is a powerful strategy for establishing the validity of a theoretical explanation (Denzin, 1989; Goetz and LeCompte, 1984; Shulman, 1988a). The application of various explanations to (in this case) the results of a study may also be considered a strategy for determining the study's comprehensiveness. A study, competently and ethically conceived and conducted, can be considered comprehensive if its results and their explanation can stand up to the challenge posed by other explanations. When researchers can demonstrate that, or explain the reasons why, other relevant explanations should be rejected, their studies are more comprehensive than when they do not.

Because the Learning to Teach Mathematics project is still in progress, we are not in a position to assess its comprehensiveness in aspects other than those already considered.

As our earlier discussions indicate, the CGI project seems to meet most of the requirements for theoretical and technical quality (Standards 1–3). Some methodological characteristics are not ideal (e.g., use of volunteer teachers; Standard 3) and the teachers' craft knowledge and the researchers' own prior commitments are not given explicit attention (Standard 1). However, overall, the study receives very high marks for clarity, coherence, and technical quality. With respect to Standard 4, the study meets the standards for external value very well, although it addresses only some of the internal value constraints. We cannot speak to the issue of balancing or trading off validity concerns, as we are outsiders to their research decisions and because no relevant information is provided in their reports (consistent with standard practice). Thus, although exemplary in most respects, CGI's overall comprehensiveness could have been improved.

Given what we have already said about Heath's work, we can summarize that although her study seems to meet our requirements for Standards 2 (cogent design) and 3 (competent application), it lacks some of the information necessary to meet Standard 1 (coherence to background knowledge). The limitation to Standard 1 in turn limits the book's ability to meet our requirements for external value (part of Standard 4) and comprehensiveness (Standard 5). Heath does not provide the information necessary to assess the study's internal value or any decisions about balancing or trading off.

CONCLUSION

In conclusion, we think that instances of valid research-based arguments in educational research, regardless of design-specific peculiarities, can take the same general form—that is, important educational issues must serve as the basis for formulating important research questions and an appropriate and ethical research design; research questions and methods must be competently linked and prior committments must be exposed; methods must be competently applied; the potential worth of the results must be weighed against the risks associated with the study; and overall, a comprehensiveness must be achieved that balances design quality and importance against risks and permits the robustness of conclusions to be assessed. As these requirements were discussed in this chapter, it should have become clear that the conception of validity we are proposing is a set of interrelated components. The five standards are not independent of each other; they cannot be applied separately. They are interrelated and must be considered together to obtain an assessment of the validity of a study.

Before closing this chapter, we would like to make one additional point, following the work of Dunn (1982). Dunn, in arguing that proposals for reform be viewed as arguments (the basis for Eisenhart and Howe's position that research studies can usefully be viewed as arguments), suggested one other metaphor: that the arguments put forward in support of and against social reform should be thought of as opposing arguments that are put forward in a court of law.

We do not think Dunn was talking about the kind of legal cases often depicted in television programs—cases portrayed as if there is one set of "objective" facts and all that is needed is a clever and persistent lawyer to discover them and make witnesses reveal them. Dunn was probably thinking more of court cases such as recent ones concerning court-ordered school desegregation in Oklahoma City (*Board of Education of Oklahoma City* v.

Dowell) or Dekalb County, Georgia (*Freeman* v. *Pitts*). In both cases, courts are being asked to decide whether school districts can be released from court-ordered desegregation plans. Arguments for abolishing court-ordered desegregation include: The District has operated in good faith for the past fifteen years, using busing, for example, to meet court-ordered racial quotas in its schools. At the same time, however, residential patterns in the city have become even more segregated, thus requiring even more busing (for example), in order to meet the quotas. Given that the schools have operated in good faith for so long and that residential patterns which are beyond the schools' control are continually increasing the costs (both financially and to the education of children) associated with meeting the court order, the schools should now be excused. In other words, it is unfair to keep the schools under court order indefinitely, especially when factors beyond their control are making it difficult or impossible to meet the requirements of the court order.

Arguments by those who want desegregation orders to remain in force include the following: The schools are an institution of society that can and should contribute to overcoming long-standing social problems, such as racial discrimination in this country. We cannot expect these problems that have existed for over one hundred years to go away quickly. Fifteen years is not a long time to wait in the grand scheme of things. Given the magnitude of the problem and the importance of addressing it, it is too soon to release the schools from any responsibility to contribute to improved racial relations.

Cases such as these have certain characteristics that provide an analogue (at least potentially) to public debate of educational issues. First, the cases have no one right, clear cut, or unequivocal answer. Second, although facts were or could be discovered (through research of some kind) and presented to support the position of each side, "facts" alone are not sufficient to decide the case. Issues of fairness, responsibility, treatment of children, importance, likelihood of success, and so forth inevitably enter in. These are the same kinds of issues that come up when the results of research are compared and in debates about the applicability of educational research findings to the improvement of practice.

Although we think the metaphor of educational debate as court of law has its limitations[6], we also think it is a very provocative way to think about educational research. If some general standards such as those offered by Eisenhart and Howe can provide the basis for establishing both the credibility and the comparability of various research studies (regardless of specific design), if use of such standards can encourage the advancement of strong arguments, and if respected panels can be found to serve as judges, then the strong results of educational research might be more widely accessible and useful.

NOTES

1. Portions of this chapter are adapted from Eisenhart and Howe (1992), and reprinted by permission of the publisher from LeCompte, M., Millroy, W., and Preissle, J., *Handbook of Qualitative Research* (Orlando, FL: Academic Press © 1992. All rights reserved).

2. Lest readers think we have unfairly singled out the work of others to scrutinize in light of standards they did not know about, see Eisenhart and Howe (1992) for Eisenhart's critical application of the same standards to her recently published work (Holland and Eisenhart, 1990) which, like the studies we describe here, falls somewhat short of the mark set by Eisenhart and Howe's standards for educational research.

3. Note that the order of the first three standards as presented here is different from their order in previous writings by Eisenhart and Howe. The original Standard 3 (Eisenhart and Howe, 1992; Howe and Eisenhart, 1990) has become Standard 1 here, and the original Standards 1 and 2 are now 2 and 3 respectively. Also, the name of the original third standard has been changed from "Alertness to and Coherence of Prior Knowledge."

4. Other interest groups or stakeholders—for example, parents, administrators—may have distinct and relevant knowledge as well [see also Florio-Ruane (1990)].

5. We will address the issue of *important* research questions under Value Constraints, the fourth standard.

6. For example, some researchers (see Florio-Ruane, 1989) object to use of the "argument" metaphor on the grounds that it implies an adversarial relationship in which one side wins and the other loses. Florio-Ruane proposes "conversation" instead. Although we appreciate the spirit of her objection, we think that conversation is too open-ended to serve as a metaphor for the kind of principled and tough debate and negotiation we think necessary for difficult and pressing educational issues; the kind of debate that results in a decision (at least a temporary one) about "what to do" in educational practice.

► 8

Good Classroom Research Is Achievable

To the reader of this book, particularly the novice researcher, the Learning to Teach Mathematics study, the Cognitively Guided Instruction project, and Heath's study may seem unattainable. Because the first two studies were carefully conceived by teams of experienced researchers and supported by grant money, and all three (especially Heath's!) spanned several years of data collection, analysis, and write up, they may appear (and reasonably so) to be beyond the reach of the prospective researcher or the concerned practitioner. However, we do not think that all "good" educational research is beyond their reach.

Although we believe that comprehensive large-scale or longitudinal research projects are, overall, the best available approach to the design and conduct of important and valuable studies that will contribute to our understanding of schools and classrooms, we also think that valuable and credible small-scale and low-budget studies are possible; they can contribute in positive ways to longer-term and more comprehensive projects. Many examples of such studies exist in the well-read pages of the leading educational research journals and on the dusty dissertation shelves of university libraries. We will discuss two such studies in this chapter—one conducted within the traditions of educational anthropology and the other within the traditions of educational psychology.

THE NARRATIVE DISCOURSE AND TEACHER KNOWLEDGE STUDY

Jan Nespor and Judith Barylske's article entitled, "Narrative discourse and teacher knowledge," appeared in the *American Educational Research Journal,* Volume 28, Number 4 (Winter, 1991). The data for this study consisted of four lengthy interviews with two classroom teachers. The interviews were conducted by Nespor, an educational anthropologist and university professor, and Barylske, a research assistant and graduate student. The original research questions for the study can be paraphrased as follows: What are the connections between the teachers' biographies and the "career structure" of the teaching profession? How do teachers, in conversations with researchers, construct representations of themselves and their conceptions of teaching? With these questions in mind, the researchers designed open-ended interview questions that encouraged the teachers to talk about "key events or experiences in the teachers' school careers, experiences that they felt had strongly shaped the way they taught" (Nespor and Barylske, 1991, p. 810), yet also allowed them considerable latitude to select what they would (and would not) talk about and how they would present themselves and their careers. After the interviews had been completed and the audio-tapes of them transcribed, the "narratives" were returned to the teachers for review, elaboration, and clarification.

Nespor and Barylske analyzed (reduced and organized) the narratives using what many would consider a "low-tech" approach. Relying on previous research results that had revealed a recurrent pattern in the stories that middle-class Americans tell, Nespor and Barylske identified each component of the pattern in the teacher narratives. The components were: the main situation or character; the emergence of a complication; and its subsequent resolution (Nespor and Barylske, 1991, p. 810). Then relying on theoretical arguments that interviews and the resulting narratives should be viewed as "socially situated," i.e., as socially purposeful exchanges, the researchers asked themselves how the teachers were crafting and using the narratives so as to develop a picture of themselves as teachers for two other adults, the university researchers.

Nespor and Barylske summarized their findings as follows:

Bob talked about his work, Clara talked about herself. Bob addressed his speech to us, constructing a version of himself as a professional teacher that situated him in between his fellow teachers and the audience of university researchers that we represented. Clara seemed to address and try to integrate the conflicting expectations of multiple interlocutors—not just us but herself and her husband as she imagined him looking at her . . . (Nespor and Barylske, 1991, p. 811).

Later the researchers continued:

Bob's account shows him . . . "enrolling" the research network, translating its interests into his own and speaking for it. His success in this . . . put his opponents in the position of having to take on the entire university-based research network if they wanted to dispute him (Nespor and Barylske, 1991, p. 813).

And,

In all of her [Clara's] accounts, family life and teaching were densely intertwined: Husband and children played critical roles as the "structuring resources" (Lave, 1988) that organized the experience of teaching . . . (Nespor and Barylske, 1991, p. 814).

Experience, in Clara's story, made research meaningful:

I think that all those things that I had learned sort of academically didn't trigger any kind of real connection with what I was doing until [she began to accumulate teaching experience], and then those things started to make sense (Nespor and Barylske, 1991, p. 817).

The researchers suggested that these differences in the biographical narratives produced by the two teachers gave them a different type of power, and a different amount of power, in the teaching profession and when talking about research or to researchers. In other words, Bob and Clara connected themselves and were connected to the teaching profession and to research in different ways. Bob was able to exert more power in his dealings with other teachers, administrators, and researchers than was Clara. Bob succeeded at this because he told his story, and in particular, he used research, in ways that are easily recognized and applauded in the dominant discourse of the profession:

Compared to Clara's discourse, Bob's narratives are more stable (being composed of discrete formulaic units), mobile (insofar as they are easier to quote and summarize), and combinable (Bob had a repertoire of stories to illustrate and support each point he wanted to make, and stories could be aggregated in support of a point, while in Clara's discourse each successive story restructured the whole in terms of which the earlier stories must be understood) (Nespor and Barylske, 1991, p. 818).

These differences make Bob's narratives more powerful in the discourse of research.

> *His relatively mobile and immutable representations of teaching and teachers are the kinds of elements with which we [researchers and some others] constitute relations of power that allow us to speak authoritatively to, for, and about teachers (Nespor and Barylske, 1991, p. 818).*

Clara's local and constantly evolving stories did not carry this authoritative power.

Up to this point, our main purpose in presenting a brief overview of how Nespor and Barylske designed their study, analyzed their data, and produced an interpretation of its results has been to illustrate its small-scale, low-budget, low-tech features. This is a kind of research study that can be done by a single researcher and with little or no grant money. (We should add that although we think this kind of research is possible without support, it is certainly preferable to have support, especially if audio tapes have to be purchased and transcribed!). This kind of research also can be done without sophisticated equipment or fancy programming skills. The study required strong grounding in the theory and traditions of a discipline and the (perhaps too often overlooked) ability to think perceptively and critically about this theory and traditions.

We turn now to questions about the quality of this study: What makes it a good study? How well does it measure up to our standards for educational research? We address these questions in two different ways. First we consider what substantive themes are reflected in the work. Second, we appraise the study in light of our standards for the validity of educational research.

As we said earlier, Nespor is an educational anthropologist; thus we would expect his work to be based on some application of ideas from the subdiscipline of educational anthropology. If we revisit the five themes identified in Chapter 4 as emerging from the previous work of educational anthropologists who study classrooms, we find that in all but one way Nespor and Barylske's study reflects these themes.

CONNECTING TO THE THEMES OF EDUCATIONAL ANTHROPOLOGY

Commitment to Culture

Nespor and Barylske used the concept of culture in a way that is consistent with recent approaches to the definition of culture. For them, "culture" includes "representational mediums" (ways of representing self, others, and the world) such as the kinds of socially situated narratives about self that Bob and Clara produced. As representational mediums, the narratives are "cultural tools" that can be selected and manipulated for their (presumed) effectiveness in social exchanges and negotiations.

Multiple Constituent Levels

The focus of Nespor and Barylske's study is narrative presentations of self as teacher. Therefore, they featured the individual level of analysis and understanding. But they did so in a way that makes culture (or the wider sociocultural system) fundamental to self: They conceive of the self—represented in the narrative—as being formed ("constituted") by the cultural tools that are available and selected for use when presenting oneself to others. Without particular cultural provisions and the social conditions that permit them to be learned and used, the self would not be constituted in the way it is. As the two teachers made use of and responded to language, imagery, and traditions to produce their narratives of self, they simultaneously defined themselves for themselves and for the researchers' understanding. In other words, the "self" is dependent upon the cultural and social contexts of its formation and use.

Differential Responses to Experiences of Schooling

The results of Nespor and Barylske's study reveal that the two teachers had very different responses to the shared experience of growing up in middle class America, to becoming teachers, and to being the subjects of a research study. They did not define or interpret their teaching experiences in the same way; nor did they use the interview setting for the same purposes.

Multiple Perspectives Represented

A theoretical commitment to distinguish the voices of the various actors (two teachers and two researchers) involved in the research process and their differential bases of power is clear in Nespor and Barylske. The researchers explicitly addressed these issues both when they introduced the study and discussed its implications. And they very clearly presented the distinctiveness of the two teachers' voices as findings of their study. However, as they noted in their conclusion, they ultimately privileged the voice of the researchers who made sense of the teachers' voices for readers of the article. Despite the inclusion of lengthy excerpts from the teachers themselves, the researchers had the final word and the privilege of connecting the teachers' "representational mediums" to their own. Interestingly, the researchers never distinguished their two voices; these remain essentially merged throughout the narrative of the article they produced.

Using Ethnographic Design

The Nespor and Barylske study is not an ethnography in the classic sense represented in Heath's *Ways with Words*. The data they used are from interviews only. The kind of interviews they used—"nondirective," meaning that the teachers were encouraged to tell their stories with little guidance or interference from the researchers—is commonly a part of ethnographic methodology but does not constitute a full-blown ethnographic study.

However, as indicated earlier, Nespor and Barylske used and interpreted their data in a distinctly anthropological way. In some anthropologists' eyes [see, for example, Wolcott (1980)], such interpretation, and not the use of particular methods, is the hallmark of ethnography. Wolcott's point is "that ethnographic techniques are necessary but not sufficient for producing ethnographic results" (Wolcott, 1980, p. 57). He continued,

> *I insist only on a clear distinction between* borrowing the research tools *so readily available and* producing the results *of those who ordinarily use them professionally.* . . . *[Those who would use the tools] must learn to* think *like anthropologists rather than simply* look *like them.* . . . *[To think like anthropologists, it is necessary] to impose a cultural framework for interpreting what is taking place. (Wolcott, 1980, pp. 57–58, Wolcott's emphasis)*

By this standard, we think Nespor and Barylske measure up.

Thus, we can conclude that although Nespor and Barylske did not use the full storehouse of ethnographic methods in their research, their perspective and approach are consistent with the four topical themes that characterize educational anthropology, and by virtue of the consistency, also with the spirit of ethnographic methodology. We turn now to a consideration of their work in light of the standards for validity of educational research that we presented in Chapter 7.

MEASURING UP TO STANDARDS FOR VALIDITY

We argued in Chapter 7 that the standards of validity are interrelated and that they must be considered as a set. However, in the analyses that follow we address them sequentially, beginning with Standard 1. We do this based on Eisenhart's earlier attempt to apply the conception of general standards for educational research to the specific case of educational anthropology (Eisenhart and Howe, 1992). At that time, she concluded that in order to determine whether the first three standards of validity were met, it was necessary to ask first, "Is there credible evidence, pursuant to the disciplinary tenets of anthropology, that data collection and analysis procedures were cogently and competently applied?" To answer this question, one had to start by identifying the disciplinary context in which the study and its methodology were conceived. In other words, one had to begin with Standard 1—awareness of and coherence with prior knowledge.

Standard 1

To assess how well Nespor and Barylske's study addresses Standard 1, we must assess how well it meets the requirements to locate the conceptual aspects of the study in existing theoretical, substantive, or explicit practical knowledge and to acknowledge the researchers' own prior knowledge or subjectivity. In this case, Nespor and Barylske clearly acknowledged and described their intellectual debt to previous writings and research regarding the cultural and social construction of knowledge and self (see again our discussion of their approach to "culture" and the concept of constituent levels). They also admitted their own subjectivity as researchers (witness their acknowledgment that they held a different power and spoke with a different voice than did the teachers they studied). However, Nespor and Barylske did not make their own orientations to, or subjectivities regarding, their research agenda clear. Thus in one sense of Standard 1 (connection to existing literature) they seemed to provide the information necessary to assess their place and contribution, while in the second sense of the standard, they did not.

Standards 2 and 3

Regarding Standards 2 (research questions should drive research design) and 3 (methods should be competently applied), Nespor and Barylske provided very little information. This too is similar to the reporting conventions that Eisenhart and Howe found characteristic of other educational research studies conducted by anthropologists (Eisenhart and Howe, 1992). As has been repeatedly observed (Geertz, 1988, *Works and Lives*), cultural anthropologists have rarely thought it necessary to provide a rationale for their choice of methods or "subjects" in the written products of their work. They also have not thought it necessary to provide detailed information about how they deployed their methods, either for data collection or analysis. Among themselves, informal standards for the conduct of fieldwork or ethnography have prevailed, and ethnographers have generally assumed that other ethnographers knew and abided by these shared norms. The accuracy of this assumption is debatable among anthropologists, but at least for educational research we think that ethnographers must make their procedures and their reasons for selecting certain procedures clearer. In the Nespor and Barylske article, we cannot tell why they chose a life history methodology. Thus we are left to wonder: Would some other method, such as participant observation, have produced different results? If so, what are the advantages (or limitations) of a life history method for Nespor and Barylske's purposes? Would use of other methods have served them better? We are also left to wonder how they chose Bob and Clara for their study, who might they have chosen instead, and what difference would a different choice have made? And finally, although we learn something about how the analysis of narrative structure was done, we are left in the dark with respect to the analysis of narrative functions.[1]

Standard 4

Our answer to the question of whether this study is worthwhile and accessible to the educational research community (external value) is a qualified yes. For one thing, we think the narratives (though substantially reduced for inclusion in a journal article) reveal teachers in ways that other teachers will recognize. Bob and Clara sound like teachers, and we think that other teachers will hear a part of themselves in Clara and Bob's words. We also expect that teachers will hear their colleagues, both those more powerful and those less so, and in so doing, will gain some insight into the status hierarchy of the teaching profession. Even the theoretical discussion, which can be quite jargon-laden and dense within the scholarship Nespor and Barylske use (social construction of knowledge and power), is (we think) quite readable and accessible. In addition, we think it is crucial for educational researchers and policy-makers to hear the distinct voices of teachers and to learn something about their worlds of experience as they portray them to others (nonteachers). If nothing else, the Nespor and Barylske article is compelling evidence of differences in the ways teachers can construe their activities and career courses as teachers and connect themselves to networks of status or power. If teachers are so different, then surely the ways in which the educational research and policy communities relate to them must be different as well. If the results of research are to appear valuable and useful to both teachers, for example, they will probably have to be presented in quite different ways!

Regarding internal value constraints, the authors provided readers with very little information. Presumably they followed standard ethical practices, such as to obtain the teachers' consent and to protect them from any risks associated with reporting the narratives. However, the article contains no evidence concerning this issue. As we have stated several times earlier, we think internal value constraints should be explicitly addressed and debated. Especially in studies like ethnographies where the research purposes and questions can change over time, we think it is very important for thoughtful researchers to discuss these constraints in their published work.

Standard 5

We find it somewhat difficult to judge the comprehensiveness of this study as comprehensiveness is discussed on Chapter 7. By definition this standard depends on a global assessment of validity in terms of the first four standards. We have already presented our position on the study's strengths and weaknesses as judged by each of these standards. Regarding the need to balance or trade off strengths in one standard against those in another, we do not have enough access to the researchers' decision-making to know whether or how well this was accomplished.

Another way to describe the comprehensiveness of the study would be to consider its potential connections to areas of scholarship beyond the particular area in which the research is located. For example, Nespor and Barylske's ideas and results might be added to debates about the role of gender and the reproduction of gender hierarchy in the teaching profession of the United States. They also might be added to debates about the roles of theoretical, empirical, and practical knowledge in teaching and for teachers. Although these areas are only hinted at in the article, they seem to us to be potential additional contributions of this small, low-cost research study. From another standpoint, however, the fact that the authors did not work harder to locate their contribution more broadly within the spectrum of educational issues may be seen as unfortunate and a limitation of its contribution.

Meeting this standard also depends on the assessment of the research community, and for that the study must stand the test of time and debate. Like many other single studies, this study, standing alone, can probably not overcome the limitations of its small scale. However, to the extent that the authors work to extend its now-limited comprehensiveness by some form of triangulation (Denzin, 1978), by successful attempts to connect their results and arguments to other areas of educational concern, and to assess these results from the vantage point of other theoretical perspectives, their overall contribution may indeed become comprehensive.

Thus overall, we are impressed with the quality and potential contribution of Nespor and Barylske's research. And they have achieved this high caliber of work in a small-scale and low-budget study that both researchers and teachers should consider accessible and achievable.

KING'S STUDY OF RECIPROCAL QUESTIONING TECHNIQUES

Alison King's article, "Enhancing peer interaction and learning in the classroom through reciprocal questioning," was also published in the *American*

Educational Research Journal, Volume 27, Number 4 (Winter) (King, 1990a). The article reports on two related studies examining the effectiveness of a guided reciprocal peer-questioning procedure for learning material presented in university classroom lectures. Each study used a pretest–posttest control group design in which the experimental treatment (guided reciprocal peer-questioning) was compared to another procedure for small group learning (discussion groups in Experiment 1 and unguided reciprocal peer-questioning in Experiment 2), and resulting student achievement was examined. We selected King's research as a second example of "doable" classroom research because, like Nespor and Barylske's study, it is a small-scale project that can be done by a single researcher with little or no support. Unlike their study, it was conducted by an educational psychologist within the traditions of cognitive psychology.

In King's words, the purposes of the first study were to:

> . . . *assess the effects of the guided reciprocal peer-questioning procedure on the quality of verbal interaction and to compare the interaction and task achievement of students using guided reciprocal peer-questioning with that of students working in discussion groups. (King, 1990a, p. 668)*

Two sections of the same education methods course were randomly assigned to the questioning and discussion conditions (one section per condition). Students in the reciprocal peer-questioning condition were provided with a set of generic question prompts (e.g., "Explain why. . . ." "How are . . . and . . . similar?") designed to elicit effective (i.e., high cognitive level) explanations. They were trained to use the generic questions, practiced taking turns asking and responding to the questions, and then used them in small cooperative learning groups following a scripted lecture on the topic of "Methods of Evaluating Student Learning." Students in the discussion condition listened to the same lecture and then discussed the material in their cooperative learning groups without receiving any guidance in discussion techniques. A pretest to assess students' lecture comprehension skills and a comprehension posttest were administered to all participants. In addition, the post-lecture small group review sessions were audiotaped and peer interactions were coded according to the following categories: giving of (high cognitive level) explanations, giving of low-level elaborations, receiving explanations, and receiving low-level elaborations. Questions were coded as either "recall" or "critical thinking."

The reciprocal peer-questioning group outperformed the discussion group on the posttest of lecture comprehension. Also, students in the peer-questioning small groups gave significantly more explanations and significantly fewer low-level elaborative responses than students in the discussion groups, received significantly more explanations in response to questions, and asked significantly more critical thinking questions. Experiment 2 was similar to Experiment 1, except that it compared guided versus unguided reciprocal peer-questioning in order to determine if the process of asking questions, in and of itself, could account for differences in verbal interaction and learning. Again, two sections of an educational methods course (this time, a different course) were randomly assigned to the two treatment conditions. Training for students in the guided reciprocal peer-questioning condition was identical to procedures followed in Experiment 1. Students in the unguided reciprocal peer-questioning condition received exactly the same training, except that they were not provided with the set of generic questions to guide their question generation. Again, a pretest of lecture comprehension skills and a posttest on comprehension of the lecture materials were administered. Also, peer interaction during the small group review sessions was audiotaped and coded.

Results were similar to those of Experiment 1. Students in the guided questioning group outperformed students in the unguided questioning group on the posttest of lecture comprehension. They also gave significantly more explanations, received significantly more explanations in response to their questions, and asked significantly more critical thinking questions and fewer recall questions than students in the unguided questioning group.

King concluded that:

> . . . the guided reciprocal questioning strategy is a way to elicit the kind of peer interaction [previous research] found effective in small-group learning, i.e., giving of high-level elaboration responses, and to discourage peer interaction found to be detrimental to learning, i.e., low-level elaboration. (King, 1990a, p.680)

Use of the guided reciprocal questioning strategy was also associated with higher performance on posttests of lecture comprehension. The generic question stems seemed to provide the guidance that students needed to generate effective (i.e., critical thinking) questions. King suggested that these question stems play an important role in facilitating learning by stimulating high-level thinking about the material to be learned. In terms of cognitive processing, the variety of questions may force students to think about the material in different ways, thus creating new links between current knowledge and prior knowledge and further elaborating their existing cognitive structures.

As we did with the Nespor and Barylske study, we now examine King's work with respect to the themes from cognitive psychological research on classrooms and the validity criteria for educational research.

CONNECTING TO THE THEMES
OF COGNITIVE PSYCHOLOGY

King is an educational psychologist who specializes in cognitive strategy instruction. Thus, we would expect her work to draw upon concepts and assumptions characteristic of cognitive psychological research in classrooms. Indeed, upon comparing these two studies to the five themes identified in Chapter 3, we find that they address all but one of the themes, at least to some extent.

The Study of Mental Events

King addressed both the content and the processes of the human mind in this set of studies. That is, she was concerned with the knowledge that students acquire from classroom lectures and with learning strategies to facilitate knowledge acquisition. Further, as she noted in the introduction to the article, ideas upon which the studies were based are consistent with information-processing theories. For example, King's treatments draw upon research which suggests that the kinds of cognitive activities in which a person must engage to provide effective explanations to another person include relating ideas to the other person's prior knowledge, noting relationships among ideas, and generating new examples (Webb, 1989). Cognitive psychologists such as Mayer have argued that these kinds of activities enhance encoding and retrieval of new material (Mayer, 1984).

Knowledge, Thinking, and Actions

The model of learning in cooperative groups upon which King based her guided reciprocal peer-teaching procedure was based on the assumption that knowledge, thinking, and actions are linked. According to that model, questions asked by one student (actions) cause the other student(s) in the learning dyad or triad to think more deeply about the material to be learned (thinking) and to provide more elaborated explanations (actions). As a result of the ensuing interactions, encoding and retrieval of information are enhanced and knowledge structures are modified (knowledge). Several of these relationships are examined in more detail in our discussions of the remaining themes.

A Focus on the Structure of Knowledge

The studies are also based on the assumptions that knowledge is structured and that learning involves modifications to one's knowledge structures. Again referring to Mayer's work, King noted that the cognitive activities hypothesized to operate when people provide effective explanations (e.g., making internal connections among ideas, making external connections between those ideas and one's previous learning) help people to integrate new information into their existing knowledge structures (Mayer, 1984). Her interpretation of patterns in the data also relates to the theme of the structure of knowledge. As we indicated above, her General Discussion of the two studies suggested that question stems are effective, at least in part, because they force students to think about the material in new ways and thereby to elaborate their existing knowledge structures.

Teachers' and Students' Cognitive Processes

The assumption that learners play an active role in acquiring new knowledge clearly undergirds the two studies. In fact, the basic premise of the research program is that some learning strategies (e.g., guided reciprocal peer-questioning, with its accompanying elaborated explanations) are more effective than others (e.g., discussion, unguided reciprocal peer-questioning) in facilitating learning from classroom lectures. Although the specific variables examined in the studies are behavioral strategies (e.g., providing explanations, asking questions) rather than internal cognitive processes, King discussed differences in the strategies in terms of the different cognitive processes they promote. She also interpreted results, such as differences in patterns of verbal interaction, as indicative of differences in internal cognitive processes. For example,

> . . . questions which require organizing the information and integrating it with prior knowledge or experience . . . [cause] the explainer to process the material more thoroughly (see Mayer, 1984). Such processing would tend to improve encoding and subsequent retrieval on an achievement test. Thus, the question stems not only affect the quality of questions asked but also improve the quality of responses given and, in doing so, influence the cognitive processing of the explainer. (King, 1990a, p. 681)

The role of the two teachers in these studies is compatible with the view that effective teachers help students to become actively engaged in appropriate learning activities. Indeed, one of the major tasks of the teachers (in addition to presenting the content lectures) was to provide training and practice in the targeted learning strategies. However, the actual cognitive processes of the teachers were not examined in the studies. Thus, we have no information about their planning for the class sessions or their thinking as they provided the training sessions or presented the scripted lectures.

The Acquisition of Expertise

This theme, that there are qualitative differences in the knowledge systems, thinking, and actions of experts and novices, is not addressed in King's research program. Nor is the acquisition of expertise an explicit focus of the studies. This topic area is simply outside the purview of King's work.[2]

Social Construction of Knowledge

As we noted in an endnote to Chapter 3, there is a growing movement within cognitive psychology to view knowledge as interactively situated in physical and social contexts, rather than existing within the mind of the individual. King's work can be considered to be a part of that movement. She sees the reciprocal peer-questioning procedure as one that provides a social context for learning and promotes the social construction of knowledge by fostering the externalization of students' cognition and encouraging the social coordination of conflicting individual perspectives.

In conclusion, although King's research does not explicitly address the theme of the acquisition of expertise, it certainly is consistent with the perspectives, concerns, and methods that characterize cognitive psychological research in classrooms. Further, it can be considered at the "cutting edge" of that research, by virtue of its attention to the social construction of knowledge. We now consider the work vis-a-vis the validity standards presented in Chapter 7.

MEASURING UP TO THE VALIDITY STANDARDS

King's studies build upon a fairly extensive body of research on the nature of peer interaction in small learning groups and its effect on student achievement. Because this is the case, we again find it most sensible to begin our assessment of the studies' validity by examining how well they address Standard 1: Contribution to the Field.

Standard 1

In the article's introduction, King did an excellent job situating the two studies in the context of existing theory and research. She showed clearly how the research questions and design are consistent with information-processing theories of learning and theories of the social construction of knowledge. She also argued effectively that the investigation builds upon the prior research of herself, Noreen Webb, and others on peer interactions in small-group learning situations, and that it extends that body of research by "modify[ing] the reciprocal peer-questioning strategy in such a way as to induce students to give explanations and other high-level elaboration responses and to determine whether they actually do so" (King, 1990a, p. 667).

However, King did not provide the information necessary for us to assess the extent to which the studies address the other components of prior knowledge. That is, she did not place the studies within the context of the craft knowledge of teachers. Nor did she discuss her own prior knowledge or subjectivity as a researcher.

Standards 2 and 3

From what we can tell based on information provided in the article, King formulated her research questions prior to designing the studies, based on the identification of ambiguities and unanswered questions in previous, related research. The design, particularly the modification to the reciprocal questioning strategy, was then derived from the questions. Further, the studies appear to have been very carefully and competently conducted, adhering closely to accepted practice within an experimental research paradigm. For example, lectures in both investigations were scripted to ensure, to the extent possible, that they were identical across treatment groups. Students were not permitted to take notes, ask questions, or interrupt the presentation during the lectures, in an attempt to control information-processing effects across conditions and to avoid confounding of note taking with treatment. Open-ended responses on the comprehension posttests and verbal interactions during small-group sessions were both coded by two independent judges. In the case of the posttests, judges were blind to student identity and experimental condition. Reliabilities were above ninety percent in all cases. In cases of discrepant posttest scores, averages were taken. All discrepancies in coding of verbal interactions were resolved by the judges. The major design limitation, noted by King herself, was the shortness of the treatment. This limitation is discussed further with respect to Standard 4.

Standard 4

As was the case with the Nespor and Barylske article, but for somewhat different reasons, our answer to the question of whether King's work is valuable for informing and improving educational practice is a qualified yes. The research certainly addressed an important problem—i.e., ways of helping students to improve their learning from lectures. The studies were fairly narrow in focus, comparing three rather specific learning strategies (guided reciprocal peer-questioning, unguided reciprocal peer-questioning, and discussion). However, because they so carefully built upon and extended prior theory and research, their contribution is greater than if they had been conducted in isolation from other research projects. King believes the studies have a contribution to make. In the final section of the article, entitled "Classroom Applications," she stated:

> *Results of these studies support the feasibility of implementing this guided reciprocal-peer-questioning and responding strategy in real-world classroom settings. Specifically, in these studies use of the strategies after the lectures was accepted as a normal part of the course, according to informal student feedback. (King, 1990a, p. 683)*

She further suggested that the strategy is applicable in a broader range of settings, including teacher-led expository lessons in elementary classrooms, use prior to instruction, and adaptation to other collaborative learning situations.

In addition, King has—at least to some extent—attempted to make her work accessible to educational practitioners. She published an article on the reciprocal peer-questioning technique in *The Clearing House* (King, 1990b), a journal written for and read by practicing teachers. Further, based on personal communication, we are aware that she is currently conducting workshops for elementary school teachers, in which she is teaching them how to use the student-generated questioning procedure when presenting lessons to their classes.

However, there is at least one major cause for questioning the contributions of the two studies reported in *AERJ* to educational practice; that is, their external validity, in the traditional sense of generalizability to "real-world" situations. Several design features, although important for purposes of ensuring internal validity, caused the class sessions and students' learning strategies to differ in important ways from standard practice. For example, based on our own experiences as university faculty members, students in higher education are well-socialized to take notes during lectures. It is difficult to imagine a naturally occurring lecture in which university students neither take notes, ask questions, nor interrupt the instructor.

A second concern related to generalizability is the limited scale in which the research was conducted. Each study included only one class per condition, and data were collected during a single class session. King acknowledged that "it is not known whether longer use of the strategy would enhance or deteriorate its effects on achievement and verbal interaction" (King, 1990a, p. 680). On the other hand, she argued, in her own previous work comprehension effects showed up after only one practice session with the guided reciprocal peer-questioning strategy and remained stable over five sessions (King, 1989). However, in that work, verbal interactions were not examined.

King provided the reader with almost no information related to internal value constraints (King, 1990a). In fairness to her, and as we have previously acknowledged, such information is rarely part of journal articles reporting on research findings. We assume that King followed standard ethical procedures for obtaining the students' consent and protecting them from any risks associated with participation or nonparticipation in the study. For example, we assume that the students' grades in the courses were in no way influenced by decisions not to participate or by their level of performance on the experimental tasks. However, the article provided no information regarding those issues or other aspects of the researcher/participant relationship.

Standard 5

With respect to comprehensiveness in the first sense—overall theoretical and technical quality—we believe that King's research holds up very well. That judgment is reflective of our assessments vis-a-vis the first three standards.

Comprehensiveness in the second sense—balancing overall technical quality with value and importance of the study—often requires tradeoffs between Standards 1, 2, and 3 on the one hand and Standard 4 on the other. That seems to be the case, at least to some extent, in King's work. As we discussed with respect to Standard 4, King sacrificed some degree of authenticity in the lecture sessions for the sake of experimental control. The extent to which that tradeoff lessens the generalizability of findings is unclear. However, certainly the issue should be taken into account when drawing implications from the research.

Finally, comprehensiveness in the third sense—attention to knowledge from traditions outside the one within which the research was conducted—is difficult to assess as it was not directly addressed in the article. However, one strength of the work is that it did incorporate perspectives from two distinct traditions—the social construction of knowledge and information-processing theories of learning. These traditions were considered in both the design of the studies and the interpretation of results. In summary, although King's work does not meet all five validity standards in an exemplary fashion, we are generally very impressed with its overall quality and its potential contribution to both theory and practice.

CONCLUSION

These studies, by Nespor and Barylske and by King, are, we think, nice illustrations of strong, credible, and useful research studies that do not require large amounts of money, long periods of time, or highly sophisticated procedures. With careful thought and planning, they and studies like them can be conducted by one person and completed in a timely fashion. We think that novice researchers are well-advised to develop their research skills by attempting such small-scale studies. Preferably, the work will be undertaken under the tutelage of a more seasoned researcher and designed to contribute to a larger program of study. Then once skills are honed, larger-scale and more comprehensive work can be undertaken.

NOTES

1. It is important to note here that Nespor and Barylske were constrained by the requirements of a journal to limit the number of pages in their article. If the field imposes a requirement that researchers more fully discuss their methodological choices, then journal editors and reviewers must provide enough space for such discussions.

2. Note that this situation should not diminish the studies' overall contribution to the literature. There is no reason that any one investigation must address all five themes in order to be judged as an excellent example of cognitive psychological research in classrooms.

▶ 9

Guidelines for
Future Research

Classroom research is important. It can illuminate classroom routines, tasks, processes, and orientations that might otherwise be obscured by the familiarity of accepted practice. It can reveal patterns in what and how children learn, in what and how teachers teach. It can inform public debate and decisions about the direction and purposes of educational reform and improvement. It can reveal how and under what circumstances teachers accept and implement the agenda of policy-makers and the public. In this book we have tried to point out some of the strengths and the potential of existing classroom research. We have also indicated some ways in which it might be improved. And, we have tried to convey some of our own experience—both the maddening frustrations and the pleasant surprises—as we thought about and conducted classroom research.

Our final purpose is to distill, from the discussions of our positions and the exemplary projects in the preceding chapters, a set of working guidelines for the design and conduct of future classroom research projects. Our hope is that these guidelines will serve as rules of thumb to encourage the production of important, useful, and technically competent classroom research in the coming years.

Guideline 1: Classroom researchers should try to design research studies that accommodate the complexity and distinctiveness of classroom life.
If, as we have claimed, the routines, tasks, processes, and orientations of classroom life are complex and interrelated, then studies of classroom life must be sensitive to this phenomenon. Classroom studies must also be sensitive to special features—including multidimensionality, simultaneity, im-

mediacy, unpredictability, publicness, and their own unique history (Doyle, 1986)—that characterize classroom life and make it distinctive. Unless care is taken to consider this complexity and distinctiveness when designing classroom studies, the results of these studies may be misleadingly narrow, the implications for practice may be overly-simplified, and practitioners may not recognize themselves or their circumstances in the research accounts they read. We think that researchers can overcome some of these problems if they design studies that explore, preserve, and build upon the actual circumstances of classroom life and practice. At this point in the evolution of educational research, we think that comprehensive research designs—designs that attempt to accommodate the complexity and distinctiveness of classroom life—are the best available means for achieving this goal.

Guideline 2: Comprehensiveness can be enhanced through efforts at interdisciplinary collaboration.
One way for researchers to expand the comprehensiveness of their research designs is to work together with other researchers who have expertise in different scholarship disciplines. We have found that interdisciplinary collaboration in classroom research requires researchers who are very clear about their disciplinary foundations, and who can articulate disciplinary commitments and recognize when to compromise them (or not) in order to address important educational issues. If theoretical or conceptual frameworks from several disciplines can be used to identify research questions, design studies, collect data, analyze the data, and interpret them, then the opportunities are increased for taking and developing a broad view of the research topic as well as the meaning and implications of the results. As a consequence, the research is more likely to address, and to inform our understanding of, the multifaceted nature of classroom teaching and learning. Although we have found interdisciplinary collaboration difficult, we have also felt rewarded by its large payoff for increasing the comprehensiveness of our studies.

Guideline 3: Research comprehensiveness, as well as the value of research for practice, can be enhanced through efforts to engage teachers and researchers in more complementary research roles.
One of the long-standing problems in educational research has been the lack of truly productive work involving both teachers and researchers. Different occupational concerns, poor communication, and status differences have tended to enforce a separation of the two groups. However, if research is to "speak" to the concerns of teachers, if it is to be sensitive to the real conditions they face, and if it is to be valuable and useful in reforming or improving educational practice, it seems to us that teachers and researchers

MUST learn to work together. We think that the opportunities for successful collaborations between teachers and researchers can be increased if both groups will commit to school improvement over the long haul, will rely on the strengths that each brings to the school improvement effort, and will agree to listen to and debate each others' views and positions. Although we expect that this form of collaboration also will be difficult, and that it will require both teachers and researchers to take on some new roles, we think that the end result will be worth the effort expended.

Guideline 4: Classroom research should be conceived in the spirit of on-going deliberation, negotiation, and decision-making by all interested parties.
Classroom research cannot be conducted according to some recipe for research design, by following a textbook definition of what to do, when, and where. Because of the many differences in classrooms and schools, variations in the concerns and perspectives of various stakeholders, and the need for meaningful research to be sensitive to these differences, research designs must be formulated and conducted in an atmosphere of flexibility, reasoned argument, and group decision-making. Notably, these features have not always characterized the educational research enterprise; we hope they will be more prominent in the future.

Guideline 5: Classroom research should be conducted in accord with some agreed-upon standards for validity.
Because of the differences referred to under Guideline 4, as well as the variety of disciplinary frameworks that might be brought to bear (see Guideline 3), educational research must proceed according to some general standards of what constitutes "good" research. The standards must be relevant and meaningful to a wide range of studies, address the values and concerns of a diverse group of stakeholders, and be respectful of the fact that good classroom research often involves trade-offs or compromises that would threaten its validity according to most textbook definitions. Without some generally agreed-upon standards for assessing classroom research, we have no way of comparing the potential of various research designs, no means for deciding what results to trust, and no consistent way to take or propose action based on research results.

Guideline 6: Classroom researchers should intend explicitly to design their research so its results can be used to address important issues of educational practice.
We have already referred to this concern in Guideline 3 and it is also incorporated into the standards for validity addressed in Guideline 5. Here we will simply stress that IMPORTANT educational issues should be the focus of classroom research. In a field where so much is at stake—the concerns of parents, the future of the country, the lives of children—and where so much

controversy exists, we think it is especially important for researchers to add the knowledge they have acquired through careful deliberation and empirical investigation to the conversation and debate about the future direction of education and schooling. We realize that implementation of this guideline is not as straightforward as it might initially seem. Different stakeholders will undoubtedly have different, sometimes incompatible, views of what constitute important issues of educational practice. However, we are convinced that when decisions about the focus of research studies are based upon mutually agreed-upon issues of importance, the contributions of classroom research to both theory *and* practice will be enhanced.

Guideline 7: Classroom researchers and teachers should make long-term commitments to the study and improvement of classroom practices.
We think that long-term commitments on the part of both researchers and teachers to the study and improvement of specific classrooms and schools are crucial if real change and improvement are to occur. The more common research practice of studying a group here and there, one practice in the first site and a different one in the second, and so forth, tends to be too fragmented in focus to assist particular teachers to make systematic and reasoned changes over time. A fragmented approach is also unlikely to produce insights useful to a wider audience, i.e., beyond the participants in the research. Further it seems to us that researchers should pay more attention to teachers' actual attempts to implement changes consistent with research results, in order to understand better the obstacles that block or subvert such implementation.

Finally, we would like to stress the special importance of reasoned debate, good judgment, and generosity toward other human beings to the success of educational, and especially classroom, research. Precisely because what occurs in classrooms is so important in so many ways and to so many people, we think it imperative that stakeholders strive to formulate, provide evidence for, and articulate good arguments for their ideas, and that they participate—as open-minded and conscientious classroom researchers, teachers, or consumers—in debates, and ultimately decisions, about how to proceed with classroom reform. Hopefully, debate and decision-making can proceed in an atmosphere of mutual respect and trust, and its outcomes supported, at least until contradictory evidence is available, by everyone involved.

In conclusion, we invite you to embark on your own programs of classroom research and improvement. We hope that after reading this book, you will have formulated some of your own ideas and developed some confidence in your own ability to conduct and contribute to classroom research. We look forward to hearing about your experiences, in your voice and with your ideas, in the future.

REFERENCES

Anderson, J. R. *The Architecture of Cognition.* Cambridge, MA: Harvard University Press, 1983.

Anderson, R. C. 1984. "Some reflections on the acquisition of knowledge." *Educational Researcher* 13 (10): 5–10.

Atkin, J. M. 1989. "Can educational research keep pace with educational reform?" *Phi Delta Kappan* 71(3): 200–205.

Barnes, D. and Todd, F. *Communication and Learning in Small Groups.* London: Routledge and Kegan Paul, 1977.

Becker, H. "Theory: The necessary evil." Paper presented at the annual meeting of the American Educational Research Association, Chicago, IL, April 1991.

Benedict, R. *Patterns of Culture.* Boston: Houghton Mifflin, 1934.

Berliner, D. C. "Implications of studies of expertise in pedagogy for teacher education and evaluation." In Proceedings of the 1988 Educational Testing Service Invitational Conference, *New Directions for Teacher Assessment* (pp. 39–65). Princeton, NJ: Educational Testing Service, 1989.

Boggs, S. *Speaking, Relating, and Learning: A Study of Hawaiian Children at Home and at School.* Norwood, NJ: ABLEX, 1985.

Borko, H., Bellamy, M. L., and Sanders, L. "A cognitive analysis of patterns in science instruction by expert and novice teachers." In T. Russell and H. Munby (Eds.), *Teachers and Teaching: From Classroom to Reflection* (pp. 49–70) London: Falmer Press, 1992.

Borko, H., Brown, C., Underhill, R., Eisenhart, M., Jones, D., and Agard, P. "Learning to teach mathematics" (Year 2 Progress Report submitted to the National Science Foundation). Blacksburg, VA: Virginia Tech, 1990.

Borko, H. and Cadwell, J. 1982. "Individual differences in teachers' decision strategies: An investigation of classroom organization and management decisions." *Journal of Educational Psychology* 74: 598–610.

Borko, H., Cone, R., Russo, N. A., and Shavelson, R. J. "Teachers' decision making." In P. L. Peterson and H. Walberg (Eds.), *Research on Teaching: Concepts, Findings, and Implications* (pp. 136–160). Berkeley: McCutchan Publishing Corp., 1979.

Borko, H. and Eisenhart, M. 1986. "Students' conceptions of reading and their reading experiences in school." *The Elementary School Journal* 86: 589–611.

Borko, H. and Eisenhart, M. "Reading groups as literacy communities." In D. Bloome (Ed.), *Classrooms and Literacy* (pp. 107–132). New Jersey: ABLEX, 1989.

Borko, H., Eisenhart, M., Hoover, N., Niles, J. and Wolfle, L. "Teaching and learning reading in its sociocultural nexus." Proposal submitted to the National Institute of Education, Washington, DC, 1981.

Borko, H., Eisenhart, M., Kello, M., and Vandett, N. "Teachers as decision makers versus technicians." In J. A. Niles and L. A. Harris (Eds.), *Thirty-third Yearbook of the National Reading Conference* (pp. 124–131). New York: The National Reading Conference, Inc., 1984.

Borko, H., Eisenhart, M., Underhill, R., Brown, C., Jones, D., and Agard, P. 1992. "Learning to teach hard mathematics: Do novice teachers and their instructors give up too easily?" *Journal for Research in Mathematics Education* 23: 194–222.

Borko, H. and Livingston, C. 1989. "Cognition and improvisation: Differences in mathematics instruction by expert and novice teachers." *American Educational Research Journal* 26: 473–498.

Borko, H. and Shavelson, R. J. "Teachers' decision making." In B. Jones and L. Idol (Eds.), *Dimensions of Thinking and Cognitive Instruction* (pp. 311–346). New Jersey: Erlbaum, 1990.

Bruner, J. *Actual Minds/Possible Worlds*. Cambridge, MA: Harvard University Press, 1986.

Byers, J. L. and Evans, T. E. *Using a Lens Modeling Analysis to Identify Factors in Teaching Judgment*. Research Series No. 73. East Lansing, MI: Michigan State University, Institute for Research on Teaching, 1980.

Cain, B. 1989. "With worldmaking, planning models matter." *English Education* 21(1): 5–29.

Campbell, D. T., and Stanley, J. C. *Experimental and Quasi-Experimental Designs for Research*. Chicago: Rand McNally, 1963.

Carpenter, T. P. and Fennema, E. "Cognitively guided instruction: Building on the knowledge of students and teachers." In W. Secada (Ed.), *"Curriculum Reform: The Case of Mathematics in the United States."* Special Issue of *International Journal of Educational Research* (in press).

Carpenter, T. P., Fennema, E., Peterson, P. L., and Carey, D. 1988. "Teachers' pedagogical content knowledge in mathematics." *Journal for Research in Mathematics Education* 19: 345–357.

Carpenter, T. P., Fennema, E., Peterson, P. L., Chiang, C., and Loef, M. 1989. "Using knowledge of children's mathematical thinking in classroom teaching: An experimental study." *American Educational Research Journal* 26: 499–531.

Carpenter, T. P. and Moser, J. M. "The acquisition of addition and subtraction concepts." In R. Lesh and M. Landau (Eds.), *The Acquisition of Mathematics Concepts and Processes* (pp. 7–44). New York: Academic Press, 1983.

Cazden, C. "Vygotsky and Bakhtin: From work to utterance and voice." Paper presented at the annual meeting of the American Educational Research Association, San Francisco, March, 1989.

Chi, M., Feltovich, P., and Glaser, R. 1981. "Categorization and representation of physics problems by experts and novices." *Cognitive Science* 5: 121–152.

Clark, C. M. and Peterson, P. L. "Teachers' thought processes." In M. C. Wittrock (Ed.), *Handbook of Research on Teaching* (Third ed., pp. 255–296). New York: Macmillan, 1986.

Clement, D., Eisenhart, M., and Harding, J. "The veneer of harmony: Social-race relations in a southern desegregated school." In R. C. Rist (Ed.), *Desegregated Schools: Appraisals of an American Experiment* (pp. 15–64). New York: Academic Press, 1979.

Clement, D., Eisenhart, M., Harding, J., and Livesay, M. *Moving Closer: An Ethnography of a Southern Desegregated School*. Final report. Washington, DC: National Institute of Education, 1978.

Clifford, J. *The Predicament of Culture: Twentieth-Century Ethnography, Literature, and Art*. Cambridge, MA: Harvard University Press, 1988.

Cobb, P., Wood, T., and Yackel, E. "Classrooms as learning environments for teachers and researchers." In R. Davis, C. Maehr, and N. Noddings (Eds.), *Constructivist Views on the Teaching and Learning of Mathematics* (pp. 125–146). Reston, VA: National Council of Teachers of Mathematics, 1990.

Cobb, P., Yackel, E., and Wood, T. "Curriculum and teacher development: Psychological and anthropological perspectives." In E. Fennema, T. P. Carpenter, and S. J. Lamon (Eds.), *Integrating Research on Teaching and Learning Mathematics* (pp. 92–131). Madison, WI: Wisconsin Center for Education Research: University of Wisconsin-Madison, 1988.

Cole, M. and Scribner, S. "Theorizing about socialization of cognition." In T. Schwartz (Ed.), *Socialization as Cultural Communication: Development of a Theme in the Work of Margaret Mead* (pp. 157–176). Berkeley, CA: University of California Press, 1976.

Colleta, N. 1976. "Cross-cultural transactions in Ponapean elementary classrooms." *Journal of Research and Development in Education* 9 (4): 113–123.

DeCastell, S. and Walker, T. 1991. "Identity, metamorphosis, and ethnographic research: What *kind* of story is *Ways with Words?*" *Anthropology and Education Quarterly* 22(1): 3–20.

Deering, P. "An ethnographic approach for examining students' aquisition of a cooperative learning classroom structure." Paper presented at the meeting of the American Anthropological Association, Washington, DC, November, 1989.

deGroot, A. D. *Thought and Choice in Chess.* The Hague: Mouton, 1965.

Denzin, N. *The Research Act: A Theoretical Introduction to Sociological Methods*. First and Second Editions. New York: McGraw-Hill, 1978.

Denzin, N. *The Research Act: A Theoretical Introduction to Sociological Methods*. Third Edition. Englewood Cliffs, NJ: Prentice-Hall, 1989.

Doyle, W. "Paradigms for research on teacher effectiveness." In L. S. Shulman (Ed.), *Review of Research in Education* (Vol. 5, pp. 163–198). Itasca, IL: Peacock, 1978.

Doyle, W. "Classroom organization and management." In M. C. Wittrock (Ed.), *Handbook of Research on Teaching* (Third ed., pp. 392–431). New York: Macmillan, 1986.

Dunn, W. N. 1982. "Reforms as arguments." *Knowledge: Creation, Diffusion, Utilization* 3(3): 293–326.

Eckert, P. *Jocks and Burnouts: Social Categories and Identity in the High School*. New York: Teachers College Press, 1989.

Eder, D. 1985. "The cycle of popularity: Interpersonal relations among female adolescents." *Sociology of Education* 58(July): 154–165.

Eddy, E. *Becoming a Teacher*. New York: Teachers College Press, 1969.

Edwards, D. and Mercer, N. *Common Knowledge: The Development of Understanding in the Classroom*. London: Methuen, 1987.

Eisenhart, M. 1988. "The ethnographic tradition and mathematics education research." *Journal for Research in Mathematics Education* 19: 99–114.

Eisenhart, M. 1989. "Reconsidering cultural differences in American schools." *Educational Foundations* 3(2): 51–68.

Eisenhart, M. 1990. "Learning to romance: Cultural acquisition in college." *Anthropology and Education Quarterly* 21: 19–40.

Eisenhart, M., Behm, L., and Romagnano, L. 1991. "Learning to teach: Developing expertise or rite of passage?" *Journal of Education for Teaching* 17: 51–71.

Eisenhart, M. and Borko, H. 1991. "In search of an interdisciplinary collaborative design for studying teacher education." *Teaching and Teacher Education* 7: 137–157.

Eisenhart, M., Borko, H., Underhill, R., Brown, C., Jones, D. and Agard, P. "Conceptual knowledge falls through the cracks: Complexities of learning to teach mathematics for understanding." *Journal for Research in Mathematics Education* (in press).

Eisenhart, M., Shrum, J., Cuthbert, A., and Harding, J. 1987. "Teacher beliefs: Definitions, findings, and directions." *Educational Policy* 2(1): 51–70.

Eisenhart, M. and Cutts-Dougherty, K. "Social and cultural constraints on students' access to school knowledge." In E. Hiebert (Ed.), *Literacy for a Diverse Society: Perspectives, Programs, and Policies* (pp. 28–43). New York: Teachers College Press, 1991.

Eisenhart, M. and Graue, M. E. 1990. "Socially constructed readiness for school." *International Journal of Qualitative Studies in Education* 3(3): 253–269.

Eisenhart, M. and Graue, M. E. "Constructing cultural difference and educational achievement in schools." In E. Jacob and C. Jordan (Eds.), *Explaining the School Performance of Minority Students: Anthropological Perspectives.* Norwood, NJ: ABLEX, (in press).

Eisenhart, M. and Holland, D. 1983. "Learning gender from peers: The role of peer groups in the cultural transmission of gender." *Human Organization* 42: 321–332.

Eisenhart, M. and Howe, K. "Validity in qualitative research." In M. LeCompte, W. Millroy, and J. Preissle (Eds.), *The Handbook of Qualitative Research in Education* (pp. 643–680). San Diego, CA: Academic Press, 1992.

Elliott, J. 1990. "Teachers as researchers: Implications for supervision and for teacher education." *Teaching and Teacher Education* 6(1): 1–26.

Emmer, E., Evertson, C., and Anderson, L. 1980. "Effective classroom management at the beginning of the school year." *Elementary School Journal* 80: 219–231.

Ericcson, K. A. and Simon, H. A. 1980. "Verbal reports as data." *Psychological Review* 87: 215–251.

Erickson, F. 1982. "Taught cognitive learning in its immediate environments: A neglected topic in the anthropology of education." *Anthropology and Education Quarterly* 13(2): 149–180.

Erickson, F. "Qualitative methods of research on teaching." In M. C. Wittrock (Ed.), *Handbook of Research on Teaching* (Third ed., pp. 119–161). New York: Macmillan, 1986.

Erickson, F. 1987. "Transformation and school success: The politics and culture of educational achievement." *Anthropology and Education Quarterly* 18(4): 335–356.

Evertson, C. M. and Green, J. L. "Observation as injury." In M. C. Wittrock (Ed.), *Handbook of Research on Teaching* (Third ed.; pp. 162–213). New York: Macmillan, 1986.

Fennema, E. and Carpenter, T. P. *Cognitively Guided Instruction: A Program Implementation Guide.* Madison, WI: University of Wisconsin, Wisconsin Center for Education Research, 1989.

Fennema, E., Carpenter, T. P., Franke, M. L., and Carey, D. A. "Learning to use children's mathematical thinking: A case study." In C. Maher and R. Davis (Eds.), *Relating Schools to Reality.* (in press).

Feiman-Nemser, S. and Buchmann, M. 1986. "The first year of teacher preparation: Transition to pedagogical thinking?" *Journal of Curriculum Studies* 18: 239–256.

Feiman-Nemser, S. and Buchmann, M. 1987. "When is student teaching teacher education?" *Teaching and Teacher Education* 3: 255–273.

Fenstermacher, G. "Philosophy of research on teaching: Three aspects." In M. C. Wittrock (Ed.), *Handbook of Research on Teaching* (Third edition, pp. 37–49). New York: Macmillan, 1986.

Finn C. E. 1988. "What ails education research?" *Educational Researcher* 17(1): 5–8.

Floden, R. E., Porter, A. C., Schmidt, W. H., Freeman, D. J., and Schwille, J. R. 1981. "Responses to curriculum pressures: A policy-capturing study of teacher decisions about context." *Journal of Educational Psychology* 73: 129–141.

Florio-Ruane, S. 1989. "Research, recalibration, and conversation: A response to Cazden, Diamondstone, and Naso." *The Quarterly of the National Writing Project and the Center for the Study of Writing* 11(4): 4–6, 24.

Florio-Ruane, S. 1990. "The written literacy forum: An analysis of teacher-researcher collaboration." *Journal of Curriculum Studies* 22(4): 313–328.

Florio-Ruane, S. and Dohanich, J. 1984. "Research currents: Communicating findings by teacher/researcher deliberation." *Language Arts* 61(7): 724–730.

Florio-Ruane, S. and Lensmire, T. 1990. "Transforming future teachers' ideas about writing instruction." *Journal of Curriculum Studies* 22(3): 277–289.

Fordham, S. and Ogbu, J. 1986. "Black students' school success: Coping with the burden of "acting white"" *The Urban Review* 18(3): 176–206.

Fredericksen, N. 1984. "Implications of cognitive theory for instruction in problem solving." *Review of Educational Research* 54: 363–408.

Freedman, S. 1990. "Research on writing and teaching writing: An interview with Sarah Freedman." *NCRTE Colloquy* 3(1): 916.

Fuchs, E. *Teachers Talk: Views from Inside City Schools.* Garden City, NY: Anchor Books, 1969.

Gage, N. L. 1989. "The paradigm wars and their aftermath: A 'historical' sketch of research on teaching since 1989." *Educational Researcher* 18(7): 4–10.

Garrison, J. 1986. "Some principles of postpositivistic philosophy of science." *Educational Researcher* 15(9): 12–18.

Geertz, C. *Works and Lives: The Anthropologist As Author.* Stanford: Stanford University Press, 1988.

Glickman, C. *Supervision of Instruction: A Developmental Approach.* Boston: Allyn and Bacon, 1985.

Goetz, J. P. and LeCompte, M. D. *Ethnography and Qualitative Design in Educational Research.* New York: Academic Press, 1984.

Good, T. L. and Brophy, J. E. *Looking in Classrooms.* Fifth ed. New York: HarperCollins Publishers, Inc, 1991.

Good, T. L. and Grouws, D. 1977. "Teaching effects: A process-product study in fourth-grade mathematics classrooms." *Journal of Teacher Education* 28: 49–54.

Griffin, G. A., Lieberman, A., and Jacullo-Noto, J. *Interactive Research and Development on Schooling: Executive Summary of the Final Report.* Austin, TX: University of Texas at Austin, Research and Development Center for Teacher Education, 1983.

Grossman, P. 1989. "A study in contrast: Sources of pedagogical content knowledge for secondary English." *Journal of Teacher Education* 40(5): 24–31.

Habermas, J. "On systematically distorted communication." In E. Bredo and W. Feinberg (Eds.), *Knowledge and Values in Social and Educational Research* (pp. 311–323). Philadelphia, PA: Temple University Press, 1982.

Hall, G. and Loucks, S. 1978. "Teacher concerns as a basis for facilitating and personalizing staff development." *Teachers College Record* 80(1): 36–53.

Hart, S. "Analyzing the social organization for reading in one elementary school." In G. Spindler (Ed.), *Doing the Ethnography of Schooling: Educational Anthropology in Action* (pp. 410–438). New York: Holt, Rinehart, and Winston, 1982.

Heath, S. *Ways with Words: Language, Life, and Work in Communities and Classrooms.* Cambridge: Cambridge University Press, 1983.

Hitchcock, G. and Hughes, D. *Research and the Teacher.* London: Routledge, 1989.

Holland, D. and Eisenhart, M. "Women's ways of going to school: Cultural reproduction of women's identities as workers." In L. Weis (Ed.), *Class, Race, and Gender in American Education* (pp. 266–301). Albany, NY: SUNY Press, 1988.

Holland, D. and Eisenhart, M. *Educated in Romance: Women, Achievement, and College Culture.* Chicago: University of Chicago Press, 1990.

Holmes Group. *Tomorrow's Schools: Principles for the Design of Professional Development Schools.* East Lansing, MI: The Holmes Group, 1990.

Hopkins, D. *A Teacher's Guide to Classroom Research.* Philadelphia, PA: Open University Press, 1985.

House, E. R. *The Logic of Evaluative Argument.* CSE Monograph Series in Evaluation. Los Angeles: Center for the Study of Evaluation, University of California, 1977.

House, E. R. *Evaluating with Validity.* Beverly Hills, CA: Sage Publications, 1980.

Howe, K. 1988. "Against the quantitative-qualitative incompatability thesis (or, dogmas die hard)." *Educational Researcher* 17(8): 10–16.

Howe, K. 1992. "Getting over the quantitative-qualitative debate." *American Journal of Education* 100(2): 236–256.

Howe, K. and Eisenhart, M. 1990. "Standards for qualitative (and quantitative) research: A prolegomenon." *Educational Researcher* 19: 2–9.

Huberman, M. 1990. "Linkage between researchers and practitioners: A qualitative study." *American Educational Research Journal* 27(2): 363–391.

Jackson, P. W. 1990a. "The functions of educational research." *Educational Researcher* 19(7): 3–9.

Jackson, P. W. *Life in Classrooms.* New York: Teachers College Press, 1990b.

Jacob, E. "Children creating culture: Cooperative learning in a multi-ethnic elementary school." Paper presented at the annual meeting of the American Anthropological Association, Washington, DC, November, 1989.

Jacob, E. 1990. "Alternative approaches for studying naturally occurring human behavior and thought in special education research." *Journal of Special Education* 24(2): 195–211.

Jones, D., Agard, P. C., Borko, H., Brown, C. A., Eisenhart, M. A., and Underhill, R. G. "Learning to teach mathematics" (Year 1 Progress Report submitted to the National Science Foundation). Blacksburg, VA: Virginia Tech, 1989.

Jordan, C. 1985. "Translating culture: From ethnographic information to educational program." *Anthropology and Education Quarterly* 16(2): 105–123.

Kagan, D. M. 1990. "Ways of evaluating teacher cognition: inferences concerning the goldilocks principle." *Review of Educational Research* 60: 419–469.

Kemmis, S. *The Action Research Reader*. Victoria: Deakin University, 1982.

King, A. 1989. "Effects of self-questioning training on college students' comprehension of lectures." *Contemporary Educational Psychology* 14(4): 1–16.

King, A. 1990a. "Enhancing peer interaction and learning in the classroom through reciprocal questioning." *American Educational Research Journal* 27: 664–687.

King, A. 1990b. "Reciprocal peer-questioning: A strategy for teaching students how to learn from lectures." *The Clearing House* 64(2): 131–135.

Kroeber, A. and Kluckhohn, C. 1952. "Culture: A critical review of concepts and definition." *Harvard University Papers of the Peabody Museum of American Archaeology and Ethnology* 47(1).

Lacey, C. *The Socialization of Teachers*. London: Methuen, 1977.

Lampert, M. 1985. "How do teachers manage to teach? Perspectives on problems in practice." *Harvard Educational Review* 55: 178–194.

Lampert, M. 1988. "What can research on teacher education tell us about improving quality in mathematics education?" *Teaching and Teacher Education* 4(2): 157–170.

Lampert, M. 1990. "When the problem is not the question and the solution is not the answer: Mathematical knowing and teaching." *American Educational Research Journal* 27: 29–63.

Larkin, J., McDermott, J., Simon, D. P., and Simon, H. A. 1980. "Expert and novice performance in solving physics problems." *Science* 208: 1135–1142.

Lave, J. *Cognition in Practice: Mind, Mathematics, and Culture in Everyday Life*. Cambridge: Cambridge University Press, 1988.

Leinhardt, G. and Greeno, J. G. 1986. "The cognitive skill of teaching." *Journal of Educational Psychology* 78: 75–95.

Leinhardt, G. and Putnam, R. T. 1987. "The skill of learning from classroom lessons." *American Educational Research Journal* 24: 557–587.

Leinhardt, G. and Smith, D. A., 1985. "Expertise in mathematics instruction: Subject matter knowledge." *Journal of Educational Psychology* 77: 247–271.

Loef, M. M., Carey, D. A., Carpenter, T. P., and Fennema, E. 1988. "Research into practice: Integrating assessment and instruction." *Arithmetic Teacher* 36: 53–55.

Mayer, R. E. 1984. "Aids to prose comprehension." *Educational Psychologist* 19: 30–42.

McDermott, R. "Social relations as contexts for learning in school." In E. Bredo and W. Feinberg (Eds.), *Knowledge and Values in Social and Educational Research* (pp. 252–270). Philadelphia, PA: Temple University Press, 1982.

McDonald, J. P. 1989. "When outsiders try to change schools from the inside." *Phi Delta Kappan* 71(3): 206–212.

Merton, R. K. "Structural analysis in sociology." In P. Blau (Ed.), *Approaches to the Study of Social Structure* (pp. 21–52). New York: The Free Press, 1975.

Messick, S. "Validity." In R. L. Linn (Ed.), *Educational Measurement* (Third Edition, pp. 13–103). New York: American Council on Education and Macmillan Publishing, 1989.

Miller, G. A. 1956. "The magical number seven, plus or minus two: Some limits on our capacity for processing information." *Psychological Review* 63: 81–97.

Moll, L. and Diaz, S. 1987. "Change as the goal of educational research." *Anthropology and Education Quarterly* 18(4): 300–311.

National Center for Research on Teacher Education. *Final Report: The Teacher Education and Learning to Teach Study.* East Lansing, MI: College of Education, Michigan State University, 1991.

National Institute of Education. *Teaching as Clinical Information Processing,* Report of Panel 6, National Conference on Studies in Teaching. Washington, DC: National Institute of Education, 1975.

Nespor, J. and Barylske, J. 1991. "Narrative discourse and teacher knowledge." *American Educational Research Journal* 28(4): 805–823.

Oakes, J. *Keeping Track: How Schools Structure Inequality.* New Haven: Yale University Press, 1985.

Oakes, J., Hare, S. E., and Sirotnik, K. A. 1986. "Collaborative inquiry: A congenial paradigm in a cantankerous world." *Teachers College Record* 87: 545–561.

Ogbu, J. *The Next Generation: An Ethnography of Education in an Urban Neighborhood.* New York: Academic Press, 1974.

Ogbu, J. 1987. "Variability in minority school performance: A problem in search of an explanation." *Anthropology and Education Quarterly* 18(4): 312–334.

Oja, S. N. and Smulyan, L. *Collaborative Action Research: A Developmental Approach.* London: The Falmer Press, 1989.

Peshkin, A. 1988. "In search of subjectivity—one's own." *Educational Researcher* 17(7): 17–22.

Peterson, P. L., Carpenter, T. P. and Fennema, E. 1989. "Teachers' knowledge of students' knowledge and cognition in mathematics problem solving." *Journal of Educational Psychology* 81: 558–569.

Peterson, P. L., Fennema, E., and Carpenter, T. P. 1988. "Using knowledge of how students think about mathematics." *Educational Leadership* 46(4): 42–46.

Peterson, P. L., Fennema, E., Carpenter, T. P., and Loef, M. 1989. "Teachers' pedagogical content beliefs in mathematics." *Cognition and Instruction* 6: 1–40.

Philips, S. *The Invisible Culture: Communication in Classroom and Community on the Warm Springs Indian Reservation.* New York: Longman, 1983.

Pressley, M., Johnson, C. J., Symons, S., McGoldrick, J. A., and Kurita, J. A. 1989. "Strategies that improve children's memory and comprehension of text." *The Elementary School Journal* 90: 3–32.

Putnam, R. T., Lampert, M. and Peterson, P. 1990. "Alternative perspectives on knowing mathematics in elementary schools." *Review of Research in Education* 16: 57–150.

Quantz, R. A., and O'Connor, T. W. 1988. "Writing critical ethnography: Dialogue, multivoicedness, and carnival in cultural texts." *Educational Theory* 38(1): 95–109.

Resnick, L. B. "Cognition and instruction: Recent theories of human competence." In B. L. Hammonds (Ed.), *Master Lecture Series*: Vol. 4 *Psychology and Learning* (pp. 123–186). Washington, DC: American Psychological Association, 1985.

Richardson, M. *Cry Lonesome and Other Accounts of the Anthropologist's Project*. Albany, NY: State University of New York Press, 1990.

Richardson, V. and Anders, P. "The role of theory in descriptions of classroom practices." Paper presented at the annual meeting of the American Educational Research Association, Boston, MA, April, 1990.

Richardson, V., Casanova, U., Placier, P. and Guilfoyle, K. *School Children At-Risk*. London: The Falmer Press, 1989.

Richardson-Koehler, V. and Fenstermacher, G. "The use of practical arguments in staff development." Paper presented at the annual meeting of the American Association of Colleges of Teacher Education, New Orleans, LA, February, 1988.

Roman, L. "Double exposure: Politics of feminist research." Paper presented at the Qualitative Research in Education Conference, University of Georgia, Athens, GA, January, 1989.

Roman, L., and Apple, M. "Is naturalism a move away from positivism? Materialist and feminist approaches to subjectivity in ethnographic research." In E. Eisner and A. Peshkin (Eds.), *Qualitative Inquiry in Education: The Continuing Debate* (pp. 38–73). New York: Teachers College Press, 1990.

Sarason, S. *The Culture of the School and the Problem of Change*. New York: Allyn and Bacon, 1971.

Schensul, J. and Schensul, S. "Collaborative research: Methods of inquiry for social change." In M. LeCompte, W. Millroy, and J. Preissle (Eds.), *The Handbook of Qualitative Research in Education*. (pp. 161–200). San Diego, CA: Academic Press, 1992.

Schlechty, P. C. and Whitford, B. L. "Shared problems and shared visions: Organic collaboration." In K. A. Sirotnik and J. I. Goodlad (Eds.), *School-university Partnerships in Action: Concepts, Cases, and Concerns* (pp. 191–204). New York: Teachers College Press, 1988.

Schwab, J. J. 1969. "The practical: A language for curriculum." *School Review* 78: 1–23.

Scriven, M. "Evaluation as a paradigm for educational research." In E. House (Ed.), *New Directions in Educational Evaluation* (pp. 53–67). Philadelphia, PA: The Falmer Press, 1986.

Shavelson, R. J., and Berliner, D. C. 1988. "Erosion of the educational research infrastructure." *Educational Researcher* 17(1): 9–12.

Shavelson, R. J., Cadwell, J., and Izu, T. 1977." Teachers' sensitivity to the reliability of information in making pedagogical decisions." *American Educational Research Journal* 14: 83–97.

Shavelson, R. J., Webb, N. M., and Burstein, L. "Measurement of teaching." In M. C. Wittrock (Ed.), *Handbook of Research on Teaching* (Third ed., pp. 50–91). New York: Macmillan, 1986.

Shepard, L. "Negative policies for dealing with diversity: When does assessment and diagnosis turn into sorting and segregation?" In E. Hiebert (Ed.), *Literacy for a Diverse Society: Perspectives, Programs, and Policies* (pp. 279–298). New York: Teachers College Press, 1991.

Shuell, T. J. 1986. "Cognitive conceptions of learning." *Review of Educational Research* 56: 411–436.

Shulman, L. S. 1986. "Those who understand: Knowledge growth in teaching." *Educational Researcher* 15(2): 4–14.

Shulman, L. S. 1987. "Knowledge and teaching: Foundations of the new reform." *Harvard Educational Review* 57: 1–22.

Shulman, L. S. "Disciplines of inquiry in education: An overview." In R. Jaeger (Ed.), *Complementary Methods for Research in Education.* (pp. 3–17). Washington, DC: American Educational Research Association, 1988a.

Shulman, L. S. "Ways of seeing, ways of knowing." In R. Jaeger (Ed.), *Complementary Methods for Research in Education.* (pp. 21–23). Washington DC: American Educational Research Association, 1988b.

Shulman, L. S. and Grossman, P. *Knowledge Growth in Teaching: A Final Report to the Spencer Foundation.* Technical Report of the Knowledge Growth in a Profession Research Project. Stanford, CA: School of Education, Stanford University, 1988.

Sirotnik, K. A. "The meaning and conduct of inquiry in school-university partnerships." In K. A. Sirotnik and J. I. Goodlad (Eds.), *School-university Partnerships in Action: Concepts, Cases, and Concerns* (pp. 160–190). New York: Teachers College Press, 1988.

Sirotnik, K. A. and Goodlad, J. I. (Eds.). *School-university Partnerships in Action: Concepts, Cases, and Concerns.* New York: Teachers College Press, 1988.

Smith, M. L. and Glass, G. *Research and Evaluation in Education and the Social Sciences.* Englewood Cliffs, NJ: Prentice-Hall, 1987.

Smith, M. L. and Shepard, L. 1987. "What doesn't work: Explaining policies of retention in the early grades." *Phi Delta Kappan* (October): 129–134.

Spindler, G. D. "General introduction." In G. D. Spindler (Ed.), *Doing the Ethnography of Schooling: Educational Anthropology in Action* (pp. 1–13). New York: Holt, Rinehart, and Winston, 1982.

Staley, F. "An ethnographic pilot study to investigate process-centered teaching." Study at Arizona State University, School Practices Laboratory, 1980.

Steward, J. *Theory of Culture Change: The Methodology of Multilinear Evolution.* Urbana, IL: University of Illinois Press, 1955.

Taylor, D. 1989. "Toward a unified theory of literacy learning and instructional practices." *Phi Delta Kappan* 71(3): 184–193.

Tharp, R. and Gallimore, R. *Rousing Minds to Life: Teaching, Learning, and Schooling in Social Context.* Cambridge: Cambridge University Press, 1988.

Tikunoff, W. J. and Ward, B. A. 1983. "Collaborative research on teaching." *Elementary School Journal* 83: 453–468.

Tikunoff, W. J., Ward, B. A., and Griffin, G. A. *Interactive Research and Development on Teaching Study: Final Report.* San Francisco, CA: Far West Regional Laboratory for Educational Research and Development, 1979.

Tobin, J. J., Wu, D. Y. H., and Davidson, D. H. *Preschool in Three Cultures: Japan, China, and the United States.* New Haven: Yale University Press, 1989.

Van Maanen, J. *Tales from the Field: On Writing Ethnography.* Chicago: Chicago University Press, 1988.

Vogt, L., Jordan, C. and Tharp, R. 1987. "Explaining school failure, producing school success: Two cases." *Anthropology and Education Quarterly* 18(4): 276–286.

Webb, N. M. 1989. "Peer interaction and learning in small groups." *International Journal of Education Research* 13: 21–39.

Weinstein, C. E. and Mayer, R. E. "The teaching of learning strategies." In M. C. Wittrock (Ed.), *Handbook of Research on Teaching* (Third ed., pp. 315–327). New York: Macmillan, 1986.

Weisner, T., Gallimore, R., and Jordan, C. 1988. "Unpackaging cultural effects on classroom learning: Native Hawaiian peer assistance and child-generated activity." *Anthropology and Education Quarterly* 19(4): 327–353.

Weiss, C. H. "The stakeholder approach to evaluation: Origins and promise." In A. S. Bryk (Ed.), *Stakeholder-based Evaluation*. New Directions for Program Evaluation, No. 17, pp. 3–14. San Francisco: Jossey-Bass, 1983.

Willis, P. *Learning to Labour: How Working Class Kids Get Working Class Jobs*. New York: Columbia University Press, 1977.

Wilson, S. M., Shulman, L. S., and Richert, A. E. " '150 different ways' of knowing: Representations of knowledge in teaching." In J. Calderhead (Ed.), *Exploring Teachers' Thinking* (pp. 104–124). London: Cassell Educational Limited, 1987.

Winne, P. H., and Marx, R. W. 1982. "Students' and teachers' views of thinking processes involved in classroom learning." *Elementary School Journal* 82: 493–518.

Winne, P. H. and Marx, R. W. "The best tool teachers have—their students' thinking." In D. C. Berliner and B. V. Rosenshine (Eds.), *Talks to Teachers* (pp. 267–304). New York: Random House, 1987.

Wolcott, H. 1980. "How to look like an anthropologist without really being one." *Practicing Anthropology* 3(1): 6–7, 56–60.

AUTHOR INDEX

SUBJECT INDEX

Academic proficiency (in development
of school culture), 44
Action system (element of students'
learning model), 28
Actions, interrelationship between
knowledge, thinking and, 25,
124
*American Educational Research Jour-
nal*, 20, 114
*Anthropology and Education Quar-
terly*, 20

Class minority students:
effect of early (home) social environment on learning and behavior, 50–54
responses to shared school situations, compared with mainstream peers 47–48
Classroom environment, distinctive
features of, 16
Cognitive psychology, 19, 23–40
cognitively guided instruction (CGI),
34–39
cognitive psychological themes
and methodological considerations, 37–39
overview of the project, 34–37
effective application of data-
collection and analysis to, 100
methodological
considerations, 31–33
as part of collaborative research used
in development of mathematics
teacher, 66–68

reciprocal questioning techniques
(King's study) and, 124–126
themes in classroom research,
24–31
acquisition of expertise, 30–31
focus on the structure of
knowledge, 25–27
knowledge, thinking, and
actions, 25
study of mental events, 24–25
teachers' and students' cognitive
processes, 27–30
Cognitively Guided Instruction (CGI)
project, 24, 34–39, 113
cognitive psychological themes and
methodological considera-
tions, 37–39
comprehensiveness of, 108–109
contrasted with *Ways with
Words*, 50–54
contribution to knowledge in the
field, 96–97
effective application of data-
collection and analysis
techniques, 101
external value constraints
addressed, 104
fit between data-collection
techniques and research
questions, 98–99
internal value constraints
addressed, 107
overview of the project, 34–37
teacher-researcher collaboration
in, 84–85

role in the research enterprise for, 81–85
    conducting descriptive research in classrooms, 82–83
    conducting intervention research in classrooms, 83–85
    identifying problems, 82
"Think-aloud" (process tracing method), 32
Thinking, interrelationship between knowledge, actions and, 25, 124

Unpredictability (feature of classroom environment), 16
Usefulness of classroom research, 75–89
    importance of teacher-researcher collaboration, 79–81
    long-term commitment to school improvement, 85–89
    role of teachers and researchers in research enterprise, 81–85
    See also Impediments to useful classroom research

Validity standards, 91–111
    approach to, 93–94
    comprehensiveness, 108–109
    contribution to knowledge in the field, 95–96
    defining, 92
    effective application of specific data-collection and analysis techniques, 99–101
    fit between research questions, data-collection procedures, and analysis techniques, 97–99

measuring up to, 126–129
    "narrative discourse and teacher knowledge study" measured against, 118–121
    reciprocal questioning techniques (King's study) measured against, 126–129
    research designed to be conducted in accord with, 133–134
    successful teacher-researcher collaboration required for, 132–133
    value constraints, 102–107
        external, 102–104
        internal, 104–107

Ways with Words: Language, Life, and Work in Communities and Classroom (research study in ethnography), 50–56
    contribution to knowledge in the field made by, 97
    external value constraints addressed in, 104
    fit between data-collection techniques and research questions, 99
    overview of the project, 50–54
    teacher-researcher collaboration in, 84
    themes of educational anthropology in, 54–56
Weaknesses of previous research, 17–18